TRAVELS
WITH
VIRGINIA
WOOLF

TRAVELS
WITH

Virginia Woolf

edited by
JAN MORRIS

THE HOGARTH PRESS
LONDON

First published 1993

1 3 5 7 9 10 8 6 4 2

First published in the United Kingdom in 1993 by
The Hogarth Press, Chatto & Windus Ltd
Random House,
20 Vauxhall Bridge Road,
London SW1V 2SA

Random House Australia (Pty) Limited
20 Alfred Street, Milsons Point, Sydney
New South Wales 2061, Australia

Random House New Zealand Limited
18 Poland Road, Glenfield
Auckland 10, New Zealand

Random House South Africa (Pty) Limited
PO Box 337, Bergvlei, South Africa

Random House UK Limited Reg No 954009

A CIP catalogue record for this book
is available from the British Library

ISBN 0 7012 0910 0

Design by Sara Robin

Filmset by SX Composing Ltd, Rayleigh, Essex
Printed and bound in Great Britain by
Butler & Tanner Ltd, Frome, Somerset

The Editor
dedicates
her small part in this book
gratefully and affectionately
to
THE AUTHOR

Contents

Introduction

This book was originally to be called *The Travel Writings of Virginia Woolf*, but the title seemed to me a contradiction in terms. Nobody was ever less of a travel writer, in the usual sense of the phrase, than Virginia Woolf, *née* Adeline Virginia Stephen. She never wrote a travel book, she wrote only a few travel essays for magazines, and in her diaries and letters she was deliberately sparing of travel reportage. Even in her youth she was wary of what she called 'descriptive writing'. It was, she wrote from Florence in 1909, dangerous and tempting:

> It is easy, with little expense of brain power, to make something. One seizes some broad aspect, as of water or colour, & makes a note of it. This single quality gives the tone of the piece. As a matter of fact, the subject is probably infinitely subtle, no more amenable to impressionistic treatment than the human character. What one records is really the state of one's own mind.

She recognised that some of the greatest practitioners – Sterne, Kinglake, Borrow, Henry James – could maintain a proper balance between description and self-revelation, but it was evidently not a skill she herself aspired to. Time and again throughout her life, especially in letters to her sister Vanessa, she cut short her accounts of places, and laughed at herself when she succumbed to the temptation of writing them, or found herself listing sights in the Baedeker manner. She much admired Kinglake's claim that his masterpiece of travel writing, *Eōthen*, was 'thoroughly free' of geographical discoveries, historical illustrations, useful statistics or political disquisitions.

All this was not only a literary distaste. It was also the fear of becoming that perennially grim figure of tourism, the travel bore. 'Travellers are the greatest bores out,' she wrote from Brittany in 1939, declining to tell her friend Molly MacCarthy 'anything about the Druids and the Carnacs', and she most decidedly never became one: everything she wrote about travel scrupulously avoids lecturing, over-detailing, hectoring or teaching grandmothers to suck eggs. 'I omit,' she wryly wrote to Molly MacCarthy after a journey to Spain in 1923, 'all about the adventures with the mule, the vulture and the wolf.'

Often indeed she deliberately avoids all mention of celebrated sights and references. She can dismiss Delphi in a few words, Rome in a page or two. She goes to Assisi without mentioning Saint Francis and Corinth apparently without noticing its canal. Although she thought of her novels in explicitly architectural terms ('built now in squares, now pagoda shaped, now throwing out wings and arcades') she rarely describes a building. She seldom embarks upon historical allusions, either, or political interpretations. I imagine that her highly political husband Leonard, with whom she did much of her later travelling, was constantly drawing social conclusions, but Virginia generally stuck to her own immediate, personal responses.

So it is above all the intimate and introspective detail that forms the substance of these writings – not at all the conventional matter of what even in Virginia Woolf's young days was gruesomely called the travelogue. Most of the extracts are from diaries and private letters, and their style shifts not only according to age, but according to context, and not least according to recipient. In writing to some correspondents Virginia sounds self-conscious, and her attitudes to places seem unconvincing. When she is writing to intimates, though, and especially to Vanessa, all is marvellously free and spontaneous, with miniatures Proustian in their evocations, flights of poetical fancy, and thoughts about place that are like entertaining footnotes, or haiku.

Virginia Woolf says somewhere that she is learning to describe things without the use of adjectives, and certainly the older she gets, the less she employs the adjectival set-pieces that are staples of orthodox travel writing. Nor does she depend in the least upon matters exciting or extraordinary – a peasant wedding was as much grist to her mill as a royal funeral, Wilton sheep fair as interesting as the Acropolis. All the same, she did once think of writing a travel book with a vengeance. 'I had an idea for a book last night,' she wrote in her diary in June 1931 – 'a voyage around the world, imaginary, hunting, climbing, adventurous people, shooting tigers, flying & so on. Fantastic.'

On the other hand the title *Travel Writings of Virginia Woolf* would also have been almost tautological, because so much of Virginia Woolf's writing is travel writing in her own kind. Few writers have ever been more powerfully inspired by the sense of place. I have included here no extracts from her fiction, but it seems to me that often the setting of her novels is at least as memorable as her characters. *Mrs Dalloway* is hardly less a portrait of London than *Ulysses* is a portrait of Dublin, and though *To the Lighthouse* is ostensibly set somewhere in the Hebrides, it is really a protracted and accurate evocation of St Ives Bay in Cornwall, with the Godrevy lighthouse on its island in the distance. Places, prospects, seas, streets, hills, the force of nature, the complexity of city life – all were essential to Virginia Woolf's art. Even *A Room of One's Own*, one of the most famous of all works of literary discussion, begins with what is in effect a long descriptive passage about the city of Cambridge.

Virginia was profoundly attached to places, especially to those she had known since childhood, and although she and her husband frequently toyed with the idea of buying houses abroad, she was really unbreakably loyal to England. As early as 1906, when she was touring Greece, she was expressing her homesickness:

It is almost strange how the longing grows & what it desires; it will feed on names, so that the simple word Devon is better than a poem; it will make pictures better than any in Greece out of a wet London street, with lamplight twisted on the pavement. . . It is not for the people we crave, but for the place. That keeps its magic; so strong that it seems to send shocks across the water.

For years Cornwall, where the Stephen family had rented a holiday home, was not only the basis of her literary inspiration, but also the criterion by which she judged all other places – the coast of Greece was compared with the Penwith cliffs, Athens inexplicably reminded her of St Ives. And it was symbolic that when she came to end her life, she should do so in the water of the English river that ran within sight of her own house, among the Sussex landscapes that she loved: the human spirit immersed at the end in the spirit of place.

Travels with Virginia Woolf it is, then, and the simplicity of the title suits the work, I think. Virginia Woolf was not a spectacular traveller, nor a natural wanderer. The romance of distant travel certainly appealed to her, and it amused her occasionally to use its idioms – camels, pyramids, porcupines, portholes, apes, caravans, gangplanks, Captains; but except for a fleeting visit to Asiatic Turkey in 1910 she never went out of Europe. She and her husband turned down a chance to tour America in 1932, apparently without regrets. 'Damn America,' she wrote, and this is how she fancied her friend Victoria Sackville-West visiting the country in the following year:

> You are . . . sitting on a tight plush seat in a car, I imagine, with views of the Middle West – an unattractive land, largely sprinkled with old tin kettles . . . The negroes are spitting in the carriage next door; and after 25 more hours, the train will stop at a town . . . you will get out, and after a brief snack off clams and iced pear drops with the Mayor, who is called, I should think, Cyrus K. Hinks . . . will go into a large baptist Hall, and deliver a lecture on Rimbaud.

She evidently had no urge, either, to visit the British territories of the east where some of her forebears had served, and where Leonard Woolf had distinguished himself as an imperial administrator. All her life she was a vigorous walker, and she made one fairly strenuous foreign journey, into the Alpujarra of southern Spain in 1923. For the rest, her travels generally took her in comfort along well-worn and limited routes.

The aeroplane had hardly come into its own in Virginia Woolf's lifetime, and hard working writer-publisher that she was, she had relatively little time for travelling. It is extraordinary now to think that this worldly, brilliant and ever-inquisitive woman never set eyes on Vienna, Brussels, Edinburgh, Munich, Geneva, any part of Scandinavia or (except from the window of a train) any mountain of those French and Swiss Alps which her father Sir Leslie Stephen, an eminent mountaineer as well as a philosopher, had famously apostrophised as 'The Playground of Europe'. She was fifty-six when Neville Chamberlain signed the Munich Agreement in 1938, and the narrowness of her travels makes one realise that he was not exaggerating when he called Czechoslovakia, hardly more than 500 miles from London, a far-away country of whose people 'we know nothing'.

Like all the intellectuals of the Bloomsbury group, whose greatest ornament she was, Virginia Woolf was in most ways extremely English. Though she was proud of an aristocratic French ancestor many generations back, she really sprang from the English *haute bourgeoisie* at the apex of its development. Bloomsbury or no Bloomsbury, she was a citizen of imperial Britain – a Victorian, old enough to remember the Queen-Empress's Diamond Jubilee, whose attitudes to abroad (as to the lower classes) were sufficiently conventional. Not a very good linguist, even she with all her genius tended to look at foreigners *de haut en bas*. Uncivilised was a synonym for unspoilt, in her vocabulary of travel, and she was not above racial generalisations, their judgements fluctuating down the years. Germans were fat brutes. Italians were charming. Greek peasants were 'far nicer' than the company the Woolfs kept in London. Though her husband was Jewish, Jews were sometimes the subjects of these surprisingly jejune pronouncements, and here is a question Virginia Woolf asked herself upon seeing a black man elegantly dressed in a swallowtail coat and a bowler hat:

> What were his thoughts? Of the degradation stamped on him, every time he raised his hand & saw it black as a monkeys outside, tinged with flesh colour within?

A little patronising, a little insensitive, when it came to travel Virginia Woolf was just another daughter of her time, class and country. Only occasionally does she feel any sense of insular inadequacy – finding her language skills insufficient for foreign conversation, or her clothes not up to foreign competition ('unreproachable, elegant and composed', she thought Frenchwomen on a train in 1923, 'while I feel like a farmyard boy who has lately rolled in the gorse bush'). She travelled only for pleasure, and she rarely travelled alone: in earlier years she was generally with family and friends, in later years with her husband. When possible she stayed at good hotels – the Hassler in Rome, the Prinz Albrecht in Berlin, the Hotel de Londres in Paris – or with hospitable English expatriots. If we had met her in a hotel lounge (she spent a good deal of time in hotel lounges) we would probably have taken her for an unusually clever but by no means extraordinary example of the English lady traveller, exchanging the usual pleasantries with compatriots before going to the escritoire in the corner to write her holiday letters home.

She liked the idea of travel, and its mechanics. She never, I think, flew in an aeroplane, and she tended to get bored at sea (though all her life she loved to watch the ships go by), but every other mode of transport seemed to please her, from the horse and carriage to the push-bike to the Orient Express to the motor car – especially the motor car, of which she became in later years, like her husband, a true *aficionado*. The car became in her mind a very engine of release, like travel itself perhaps.

The Woolfs bought their first car in 1927. It was a second-hand Singer, price £275. Virginia never learnt to drive properly, leaving that to Leonard, but she was delighted by the car – 'a nice light little shut up car . . . very dark blue with a paler line round it', which would 'expand that curious thing, the map of the world in one's mind'. All images, she wrote, were now 'tinged' with motoring. 'What I like . . . about motoring is the sense it gives one of lighting accidentally, like a voyager who touches another planet with the tip of his toe, upon scenes which would have gone on, have always gone on, will go on, unrecorded, save for this chance glimpse' – exactly the sensation, in its brightness and transience, that her topographical writing throve on.

By 1929 they had moved on to a coffee-and-chocolate-coloured Sun Singer, and by 1935 they had a silver-green, fluid flywheel Lanchester 18, smooth as an eel, Virginia claimed, fast as a swift, powerful as a tiger and sealed like a Pullman coach, which made her feel 'rich, conservative, patriotic, religious and humbuggish'. Probably the happiest of all her journeys were her motoring trips through France with Leonard. 'This is the way to live,' she wrote to Vita Sackville-West from Orange in March 1928. 'Driving all day; an hour or two for lunch; a few churches perhaps to be seen; one's inn at night; wine, dinner; bed; off again . . .'

Even so, she generally found the journey out a good deal more enjoyable than the long journey back, and at the end of her holidays she was quite ready for home. It would be a long time, she confided to her diary in Chartres in May 1935, before she went motoring again.

> The pane of glass that is pressed firm over the mind in these travels – there I am vitreated on my seat – cant read talk or write – only look at the endless avenues – plane trees poplars – rain, rain – old man with a cart – ask the mileage – look at map light a cigarette . . . all this makes the last 2 days as intolerable as the first two are rapturous.

We all know the feeling, just as anyone who lives in Britain shares Virginia Woolf's periodical pinings for somewhere brighter and warmer. Her eyes were 'grey with England', she wrote to Gerald Brenan on Christmas Day, 1922, and she wanted to feed them on country colourful and craggy – 'not perpetually sloping and sloppy like the country here'. She often considered becoming an expatriate, at least for part of the year. When Vanessa and her lover Duncan Grant set up home among the vineyards of Cassis, along the coast from Marseilles, the Woolfs set about acquiring a house there too, but this came to nothing. As did their passing enthusiasms for settling, at one time or another, in Tuscany, Avallon, Rome, Spain or County Cork, and Virginia's not very serious proposal that their Hogarth Press should transfer its operations to Crete.

Like most travelling Britons too she thought a lot about food and drink. Leonard was sometimes inclined to think that French food was no better than that at the White Hart Inn at Lewes in Sussex, his benchmark of gourmandise, but Virginia seldom agreed, and loved her foreign victuals, especially after the internal combustion engine had so widened her choice and her experience. 'Suppose one had wine every day, at every meal,' she wrote from France in 1928 – 'what an enchanted world!'

She was happy when she was travelling. Her life was full of sorrows, and much of her work is streaked with a sense of sadness, but the dominant mood of this book is one of *joie de vivre*. Occasionally one does sense, in a particularly intemperate response, or a cruel turn of phrase, hints of the recurrent insanity which burdened her life and hastened her death: it jars when she talks of elderly golf-playing spinsters who 'have no reason to exist in this world or the next', or dwells upon the ugliness of poor Londoners, or grotesquely describes the Apennines as 'bald-necked vulture country'. She witnesses some grim scenes, has her moments of boredom, revulsion and regret. Mostly, though, her travel writing is terrific fun. Not many of these extracts were written for publication, and they are above all a record of pleasures. They are however the work of a genius, and even in this easygoing literary form the genius shows.

'What one records is really the state of ones own mind.' Precisely that is the fascination of these writings. They are seldom descriptions of place, they are records of the effect of place upon a particular sensibility, one of the most finely tuned imaginable. The earliest piece here was written in 1897, when the writer was fifteen, the latest in 1940, when she was fifty-eight, and there is inevitably a vast difference in the style and approach – the earliest extracts, being hardly more than juvenilia, can be embarrassingly florid. What does not change, though, is the sensibility. People sitting in hotel lounges – overheard snatches of conversation – the light on top of a London bus – shadows in an orchard – music through a window – almost from first to last, these are the kind of things which, seized, subtly transformed, sometimes exaggerated, become quintessentially Woolfian passages.

The book should never be put on a travel writing shelf. The reader will learn very little about the countries Virginia visited, and that little is often misleading. What is displayed here is one of the fundamental influences that have moulded the gifts of a great writer, and unless one has read the novels one would hardly guess from these carefree extracts how important that influence was – that sense of place, I mean, which, distilled into something far grander than mere gossip or entertainment, elsewhere colours her art more sombrely.

'Am I not burdened?' she wrote heart-rendingly in *Poyntz Hall* (later to become *Between the Acts*), which she finished a month before her death:

> The last little donkey in the long caravanserai crossing the desert? Burdened with bales roughly bound with thongs? my memories, my possessions. What the past laid on my back; saying little donkey, kneel down, kneel down. Fill your paniers. Then rise up, little donkey, and go your way, burdened, with litter, possessions, dust and jewels, till the heels blister and the hoofs crack . . .

There are no such terrible metaphors of travel in this anthology. Virginia's latent madness seldom shows here, her resentments of gender are put aside. What travel gave one, she wrote, was a series of gradually diminishing scenes, and they were cheerful scenes that she cherished. 'One night,' she wrote in Sussex in 1929, 'I had that curious feeling of being very young, travelling abroad, & seeing the leaves from a train window, in Italy – I can get the feeling right now. All was adventure & excitement.' Virginia Woolf greatly enjoyed her journeys, home or away, and half a century after her death her pleasure remains with us, in these miscellaneous memoirs of movement and observation, as a mostly merry legacy of a grand but tragic life.

A Note about Usages

🐦 In editing this book I have generally called Virginia Woolf 'Virginia', because although it sometimes sounds ingratiating and sometimes patronising, it seems to me better than any of the alternatives.

🐦 I call something a journal, rather than a diary, when it is not dated daily, but is a record of a period.

🐦 I have generally tried to print extracts in chronological order, but have sometimes lapsed for aesthetic reasons, or for clarity's sake.

🐦 Spelling and punctuation I have left as they are in previously published collections of Virginia Woolf's diaries, letters and essays, prepared by more scholarly editors.

Itinerary

HOME

Itinerary

AWAY

Home

Home was always England. Virginia Woolf's life lasted fifty-nine years, and all but some eighty weeks of it she spent in her own country. Her attachment to England was profound without being ostentatious (patriotism was suspect in Bloomsbury) and time and again she expresses it in snatches of diaries and letters. 'This is far the loveliest country in Europe,' she exclaimed in 1916 (having by then seen eight of the others), and in 1935 she was still declaring it 'now and then the most poetic of all countries'. Was she not, after all, elected in the last year of her life Treasurer of the Rodmell, Sussex, branch of the Women's Institute? What could be more English than that?

London

Virginia Woolf was always a Londoner. Though she eventually made her principal home in the country, she constantly returned to the capital, often wrote about it and remained its affectionate citizen. She was born in 1882 at 22 Hyde Park Gate, a cul-de-sac of large Victorian houses off the Kensington Road, and spent the first twenty-two years of her life there. Between 1904 and the end of her life she lived at eight other London addresses: in Gordon Square, Fitzroy Square, Brunswick Square, Clifford's Inn, The Green at Richmond, Hogarth House at Richmond (where she and her husband Leonard Woolf established The Hogarth Press publishing house), Tavistock Square and Mecklenburgh Square. As a child, suffering the first symptoms of madness, she had sometimes found the life of the city sinister and frightening; in her maturity she loved to wander its streets alone – 'to walk alone in London,' she wrote in 1930, 'is the greatest rest.'

Her evocations of London life run from the turn of the century to the Second World War.

'Remembering Hyde Park Gate'
A paper read to the Memoir Club in the early 1920s

Hyde Park Gate, which led nowhere, but made a little

sealed loop out of the great high road running from Hammersmith to Piccadilly, was something like a village street. One heard foot steps tapping along the pavement. Most of the people bowed to each other as they met. One recognized them approaching. That was Mrs Muir-MacKenzie; handsome, distinguished. That was the pale Miss Redgrave; or that was the red-nosed Miss Redgrave; or that was the ancient Mrs Redgrave, veiled in widow's weeds; going out in her bath chair with a Miss Redgrave in attendance . . .

Everybody knew everybody, and everything about everybody, in Hyde Park Gate. It was a trial, if you disliked the gradual approach of a familiar face as I did, to see the MacKenzies or the Redgraves coming nearer and nearer until you had to stop or at least smile. The houses were all individual houses; some towering high, like ours; others, like the Redgraves', long low houses almost country houses; some had strips of garden; others were flush with the street. But they had become stereotyped, pillared, and pompous up at the top fronting the main road. Incredible as it now seems, I can remember that one of these pompous houses had a carriage and pair with a coachman and a footman who wore powdered wigs, and yellow plush knee breeches and silk stockings. Yet the owners were of no particular importance; and yet nobody thought such magnificence was strange. Perhaps one house out of every six in Hyde Park Gate kept a carriage, or hired one from Hobbs whose livery stable opened its great yard in the middle. For there was only the red bus to take people 'into Town', as father called it, or, if you could afford it, a hansom or four-wheeler from the rank. The underground, a sulphur smelling steam clouded tunnel with trams running, I suppose, rather seldom, was far away . . .

The streets were full of horses. The streets were littered with little brown piles of steaming horse dung which boys, darting out among the wheels, removed in shovels. The horses kicked and reared and neighed. Often they ran away . . . horses went sprawling; they shied; they reared; wheels came off. The street rocked with horses and smelt of horses. The horses were often gleaming, spick and span horses, with rosettes in their ears; the footmen wore cockades in their hats; foam flecked the bright silver harness; coronets and coats of arms were painted on panels and among the sounds of the street – the tap of hoofs, the rush of wheels – one heard a jingling and metallic noise as the harness shook and rattled. But only solitary hansoms, or little high butchers' carts, or private broughams came clopping down our quiet Hyde Park cul-de-sac.

We are told that nearly a score of the nineteenth-century inhabitants of Hyde Park Gate are listed in the Dictionary of National Biography *(whose first editor was Virginia's father, Sir Leslie Stephen). Later the street was to become even more distinguished, for it was at Numbers 27 and 28, knocked together into one house, that Sir Winston Churchill died in 1965. Number 22 is now marked by a plaque commemorating Sir Leslie, but not his daughter. The street is confusing, for it is no longer a loop, but is divided into two separate parts both called Hyde Park Gate. Virginia's part is still largely residential, some of its buildings being 'pillared and pompous', some very expensive modern houses, but it also includes the Fijian Embassy, an institution inconceivable in her time. Other residents remembered by blue plaques are Jacob Epstein the sculptor and Robert Baden-Powell the original Boy Scout.*

Victoria's Diamond Jubilee
Diary, 22 June 1897

Today was the great Diamond Jubilee Day, very cloudy & still early in the morning, looking almost showery if such a thing dared happen . . . We got to St Thomas'es Hospital at 9.30, & watched the soldiers & the crowd for some time. There the crowd was not allowed on the [Westminster] bridge, & we had nothing but lazy volunteers to look at. So we strolled in the hospital gardens & had ices . . . At 12.30 a

Captain Ames, & the sailors appeared & then followed troop after troop – one brilliant colour after another. Hussars, & Troopers & Lancers, & all manner of soldiers – then Indian Princes, & at last carriages with the little Princesses & the big ones – Finally the cream coloured ponies were sighted: every one stood up & waved: shook their pocket handkerchiefs, & stamped their feet – the Queen was lying back in her carriage, & the Pss. of Wales had to tell her to look up & bow. Then she smiled & nodded her poor tired head, & the whole thing moved on.

The 50,000 troops in the Jubilee procession were said to constitute the largest military force ever assembled in London, and Captain Oswald Ames of the Life Guards, who led the half of it that Virginia Woolf saw, was at six feet eight inches the tallest man in the British Army. The poor tired Queen-Empress was in her seventy-ninth year.

An Artistic Party
Diary, 1 July 1903

Again we took [a] cab tonight & drove through the populous streets which look their gayest about this hour. We had four large cards for the Academy Soirée – an entertainment unique, I should think, of its kind . . .

The Academy is a gloomy place, even on its festive nights; you take off your cloak in a kind of catacomb, damp, with stone arches. The little urbane President, already looking a trifle bored, pressed our hands perfunctorily & we passed on into the great rooms. This crowd, I say, has a character of its own. Every other person you feel must be distinguished: the men wear a surprising number of decorations – Bath ribbons & stars & all kinds of humbler orders – so we decided when we saw their dress clothes (a rude test of merit!)

The women, as though to atone for their want of definite orders, dress up in the oddest ways. We found

some queer specimens. Here was a stuffy black dress, somehow suggestive of high tea & bugles; here the artistic
temperament had gone to the other extreme, & left bare a
good deal of the person which is usually covered. But the
most usual figure was the typical artist, or artists wife –
clinging Liberty silks – outlandish ornaments – a strange
dusky type of face. Of course there were too others like
ourselves, of no particular description. Still I could have
been well content to take my evening's pleasure in observation merely. I was constantly starting at some face well
known in photograph or caricature suddenly fronting me
in the life. I was constantly wishing to point – with extended forefinger – at some delicious discovery, male or
female, till they were too frequent to need remark –

It is not a party at which one talks. The conditions are
somehow adverse. The great rooms indeed are full, but you
never rid your mind of the public gallery feeling – & certainly the light & space are not becoming. The crowd as a
whole looks badly dressed, & moves awkwardly. Its units
never seem to dissolve & melt together. We drifted about,
gazing at human pictures mostly, with snatches of desul-
tory talk. We looked with admiration at those ladies, who
are the high aristocrats of such gatherings as these – who
know the President & all the more distinguished academi-
cians. Their demeanour is beautiful. Exquisite in old lace &
most refined evening gowns, they know well that they are
the Queens of the gathering. What they are, everyone else
desires to be – at least this evening. They bear names as
famous in the world of art as Russell & Cavendish in the
world of fashion. I am always impressed by the splendid
superiority of these artist men & women over their Philis-
tine brethren. They are so thoroughly convinced that
mankind is divided into two classes, one of which wears
amber beads & low evening collars – while the other follows the fashion. Each thanks God that it is not as the other
– but the artist is the more intolerant. We must have past
through all the rooms, & we began to get tired of human
faces.

A cab home again! Down the brilliant charging Piccadilly, now thoroughly awake, as though it had slept all day.
The wood pavement in the heat gets beaten to a shiny hard
surface, which at night reflects the lamplight almost as
though it were wet.

*The President of the Royal Academy then was Sir Edward Poyn-
ter. Russell & Cavendish were not a smart department store, but
the family names respectively of the Dukes of Bedford and Devon-
shire. The Academy's annual reception is very much the same
today, eleven Presidents later.*

An Expedition to Hampton Court
Diary, 5 July 1903

Most Londoners have travelled in Italy – Turkey or Greece
– they run to Paris or Scotland almost for the week end –
but, judging from my experience, the immediate neighbourhood of London itself is an unexplored land. On their
map it might be marked blank like certain districts of Africa.
It is sober truth that though I have lived my life in London I
have only once visited Hampton Court. Kew, Richmond,
Hampstead, I know a trifle more familiarly perhaps –
Various causes make it easier to go anywhere almost than
to the suburbs of London. You have to make a days expedition; no one that I am aware ever sleeps at Kew or
Hampton Court. They are essentially places which you visit
between trains. You find yourself with a summer afternoon
to spare – bethink you that you really ought to know these
places a little better, & thus once in a dozen years you find
yourself much to your surprise walking in the Orangery at
Kew or treading the maze at Hampton Court. I am always
surprised – pleasantly surprised to find myself here. Nevertheless I let years slide, & bear me to all quarters of England,
before I go there again. The summer afternoon never
comes – anyhow you spend it in the Gardens which lie at
your gates. This occurs to me because today we have

actually achieved the task: we have been to Hampton
Court. It is true we planned the journey for a year – twelve
perhaps will pass before we set about to plan another – but
I write today with absolutely first hand knowledge. My information is crammed from no guide book or travellers
tales. I have seen what I describe with my own eyes.

We started, then, at 11. The journey to Hammersmith
really presents no scene worthy of description; besides it is
comparatively hackneyed ground. It is after one has left
Hammersmith that one enters strange land. The street
begins to look far more like a village street; the houses are
of a far more individual character, & they have space in
which to expand. But yet it has marks of belonging – of
being a distant though poor connection of a great town.
You get an impression that the more respectable classes of
London have retired here to pass their old age with greater
dignity & peace than they can afford inside London itself.
Piety has retired here too; I counted a surprising number of
Convents & Sisterhoods as we went along; once or twice to
my pleasure I could look down into their cloistered grounds
& see the sisters themselves walking there – Once I spied
into the garden of an orphanage for Roman Catholic little
girls. The children were all ranked in two & two, following
a dark sister in some kind of procession, & they all, for what
reason I do not know, wore wreaths of white flowers round
their heads – an innocent sight truly, as one passes. Then
one began to catch glimpses of the river through steep little
alleys which opened out of the main road, & once we came
upon a whole fleet of barges moored together for the Sunday rest as we past over the bridge. The picturesque
bargeman was removing a weeks cole grime on deck – his
head buried in a basin, & white with lather. This was in
Brentford I think, but to tell the truth I have no notion
what villages we past through or in what order they came.
They were not separated from each other, though
originally as distinct as London from Birmingham. Nevertheless there were very few new buildings. Most must have
been 60 or 70 years old I should think, & a common type

was the pleasant square Georgian house. This must originally have stood in a space of its own, I am sure; Georgian houses were built for opulent people, who could afford light & air – At any rate the whole road to Hampton Court which it took us an hour & a half to travel, was well worth looking at. At half past one, at last, we reached our journeys end. In a moment we were walking the broad terrace of the Palace Garden. My one visit ten years ago, had not left in my mind any adequate picture of the beauty & space of this old garden. I had forgotten too the richness of the dark red palace itself. At first I felt simply inclined to pace slowly up & down the terrace & let my eye rest first on the smooth turf lit by brilliant flowers, then on the perfectly satisfying shape of the palace. But it was cold, & we were hungry, & somewhat to our surprise, half London apparently had had the same idea of visiting Hampton Court at the same day & hour as we had. The terraces & the turf which I felt ought only to have been peopled by ladies in brocade & gentlemen in kneebreeches & swords, swarmed with a very different class of person – perhaps more moral than their ancestors of Charles 2nds time, but in penalty for it far less ornamental. I could not help regretting the improvement in morality. I wished again & again – so did the whole crowd of us, I daresay, that I could have had those gardens to myself. They are meant for peace & luxurious meditation. We lunched – with our fellows – Everywhere we went it occurred to several dozen others to go too. I must retract what I said to begin with – that Cockneys dont go to Hampton Court. But doing our best to think ourselves alone, we strolled through the quadrangles after lunch. They are, I imagine, perfect of their kind: Oxford & Cambridge can show no better. Absolutely no alteration, no restoration, as far as one can see, has touched these old buildings since the careful hand of the Architect laid stone to stone. The difficulty was – not to imagine Charles & Nell Gwynn idling there with voluptuous Court ladies lounging after them, but to remember that we who walked there were absurdly & monstrously out of place. We paced the galleries. Here indeed the illusion so strong on one in the courts & gardens gave way almost entirely. These beautiful old cedar lined rooms which run all round the quadrangle have had their walls so papered with pictures that their domestic character has disappeared. Some of the paintings indeed are first rate – some bad – but good or bad they make the place into a public gallery where one goes prepared to take in instruction & pleasure, catalogue in hand. The rooms indeed have their old uses inscribed on them – Queens Bedroom – Queens private drawing room – Kings ante-chamber &c – but it is not possible to reconstruct them in your mind as they were then. Yet Henry the 8th walked here – & the little Edward the Sixth was brought here to die, I think, & wits & beauties without end have past through these rooms, all of which one might have revived in ones mind, if the old chairs & tables had been left in their places.

After we had done our duty here, we spent an hour or so wandering through the gardens again, finding our way down to the lake side where we lay & watched an appropriate pair of anglers. They, like a sundial, are absolutely essential in a picture of this kind; the fish is never caught, the angler dreams away the whole length of the golden hours – that is a pursuit which like the registering of sunbeams, belongs to a less machine driven, & sunnier age than ours.

But we had overstayed our time already. It seemed absurd to be bound by ties made so far away – almost in such a different age, but long ago in London we had promised to come home for tea. That was impossible. If we strolled peacefully back, we should return in time for dinner. Most of our companions had exhausted their interest in Hampton Court. They had had an outing which they had enjoyed energetically, & were now eager to get home again. We had the darkening garden almost to ourselves as we walked across it, but in the dark we could see one or two dignified figures moving up & down the terrace as we passed. It was impossible to mistake them. They were no cockney trippers making the whole place hideous with their noise & Cockney faces; no, these Ladies are part of the palace. They belong to it. It is admirably appropriate I think that our aged aristocracy which finds no home in the bustling town, should retire to spend its last days in this old Palace full of tradition & ancient splendour – splendour even more beautiful I should think in its mellow age than in its prime. These old Ladies with their great names & bent old bodies stay in my mind as the very spirit of the place, which we surprised haunting the walks by dark. Here they dwindle out their old age, as in some royal almshouse. No retirement could be sweeter or more dignified than to this Palace by the Thames.

Even in 1903 Virginia Woolf could have got to Hampton Court in forty-five minutes on the South Western Railway from Waterloo (fares, the Baedeker of the day, says, 2s., 1s. 6d., 1s. 2½d., the ride affording 'a charming and thoroughly English picture'). Her road journey, evidently via Chiswick, Brentford, Richmond and Kingston upon Thames, would be almost unrecognisable to her today – no coal barges, few convents, hundreds of thousands of new buildings and the flight path to Heathrow Airport overhead. Part of Hampton Court was destroyed by fire in 1986, but it has all been restored, and once again looks more or less as 'the Architect laid stone to stone'.

At the Fun Fair
Journal, 22 July 1903

We go once a year to Earl's Court [exhibition and fun-fair]. I do not know that I want to go oftener – but I enjoy that one visit. This evening . . . the first thing we made for was the Chute . . . The Chute is unfailing: I tremble to think what my state of mind will be when I fail to appreciate the Chute. And yet last year I made six descents running without any hesitation, & this year I didn't mind stopping after the third . . . Each time we got a front seat – rushed down, with the usual shrieks & blowing hats, plunged into the water, reared up, & then wobbled back to shore — There was some difficulty in deciding what to do after this — but 'The River of Lava' written in twinkling lamps attracted Adrian [her younger brother] & me so much that we paid our sixpences & took our seats in the boat. It was a horrid fraud . . . The point is that you are floated along a kind of drain which is worked by electricity so that the current floats you without oars. The way is variegated with grottos & sunsets & effects of light upon the water — but we all agreed it was a very bad show . . .

We wandered through a most perplexing number of courts all with bands in the centre & outlines of electric light, & crossed bridges & looked at any number of side shows, or their signs, which are perhaps more amusing. The showmen were expounding the merits of their marvels & mysteries in the spirit of purest philanthropy . . . We were terribly tempted by Spiders web — which is the sensation of America — by the upside down House, by various magicians & palmists. Adrian however was no longer to be restrained when we came to a tent in which for the paltry sum of sixpence you could enjoy a musical ride upon absolutely real live horses . . . He mounted: his piebald at the sound of a whistle & the tinkle of a musical box, started pacing round the circle — really no bigger than this room. Half a dozen other drugged looking ponies joined, ridden by a disagreeable shopkeeper & hairdresser who though they stuck to their saddles with some difficulty were always beating their beasts to go faster.

A woman dressed in a scarlet habit — if it can be called by so definite a name — circled round too. A lady in a short black shirt & a blouse jolted at the head of the melancholy procession, but, after cannoning several times with the rider behind, she thought she had had enough of it and dismounted. Meanwhile Adrian plodded steadily round — the most comic sight in the world. I thought the ponies would never have the strength to stop once they had begun — but a whistle sounded & they came to an end, more than anything else, in the middle of their stride. If it hadn't been so indescribably dingy, & degrading for any live creature, I could have laughed at the sight; I did laugh in fact – but nevertheless it was a depressing side show on the whole. As we left, a man came up & entreated us to laugh a hundred times for sixpence – All we had to do was to pay our six-pence & walk inside. It was such a generous offer that we accepted. Inside we found ourselves in a tent lined with looking glasses, of all conceivable curves & hollows: we grew long – & lop side & gigantic & dwarfed. Our bodies were twisted every possible way till finally we were repre-sented by a pair of legs only. When we felt we had secured as many of our 100 laughs as were forthcoming we left. The exhibition closes at past 11 & till then we sat beneath a band & listened to popular tunes. We shall not go to Earls Court again for another year.

The annual Earls Court exhibitions, which began in 1887, took place on a fairground on the site of the present exhibition hall, which was opened in 1937. The 'Spiders web' seems to have been the Ferris Wheel, created for the Chicago World's Columbian Ex-position, ten years before, in emulation of the Eiffel Tower which had been built for the Paris Exposition of 1889: in America it was called 'a bridge on an axle', and its classic progeny is the Big Wheel in the Prater at Vienna (1896).

By Tube to Golders Green
Diary, July 1907 (undated)

The Twopenny Tube has now burrowed as far as Golders Green; so that sinking into an earth laid with pavement & houses at one end, you rise to soft green fields at the other; the ashen dark & the chill & the cold glitter of electricity is replaced by the more benignant illumination of daylight. Indeed on Sunday there was a sky & a sun; & the exuberant holiday making of the crowd had some excuse. Well, we all of us got out at Golders Green; which term I take to apply to a dusky triangle between cross roads, which was now occupied by a cluster of idle people sucking like bees at some gaudy & profuse flower. Their little island was a refuge from motor cars which shot past constantly almost shaving slices from the edge . . .

Golders Green is all red brick; huge factories of railway buildings are especially prominent; then to the North (perhaps) there was another separate hamlet, grouped as real villages are up a hill which was pointed by a Church spire. And between them there was this soft land, undulating with long grass & curving into little mounds . . . Old lichen crusted palings, & streamlets & fields with cows in them, all seemed ready to prove that they were part of the neglected world, & then the tail of your eye was caught by a line of villas, like a block of childrens bricks set on end. A line of moving heads at a little distance showed me that there was, as I expected, a regular channel up to Hampstead, along which one might legitimately walk . . .

It had been but a short time before, a foot path; & the glamour of the afternoon to me was caused by the fact that it led us past a real country farm, with a yard & a dog; I looked in at the window & saw the family at dinner, & there was a stuffed jay in a case.

The Twopenny Tube was the Central London Railway, which had a flat fare of 2d., but it was the Hampstead Tube which had just tunnelled under Hampstead Heath to reach the fields of Golders Green – the line had been opened a month before by David Lloyd George, President of the Board of Trade. Golders Green (in whose rural crematorium Virginia's father had been cremated in 1904) was not to keep its cows for long: all was soon enveloped in suburban development, and between the world wars the district became a chief sanctuary for Jewish refugees from Europe.

War I

For a long period during the First World War Virginia Woolf was unable to write because of her mental condition. The diary notes she did leave give a curiously mixed picture of life in wartime London.

Went to Days, to get more books. Days at 4 in the afternoon is the haunt of fashionable ladies, who want to be told what to read. A more despicable set of creatures I never saw. They come in furred like seals & scented live civets, condescend to pull a few novels about on the counter, & then demand languidly whether there is *anything* amusing? The Days' assistants are the humblest & most servile of men – They tow these aged Countesses & pert young millionairesses about behind them, always deferential, & profuse of 'Ladyships'. The West End of London fills me with aversion; I look into motor cars & see the fat grandees inside, like portly jewels in satin cases.

Diary, 13 January 1915

Day's was a circulating library in Mount Street, Mayfair.

We took a tram to Kingston & had tea at Atkinsons, where one may have no more than a single bun. Everything is skimped now. Most of the butchers shops are shut; the only open shop was besieged. You can't buy chocolates, or toffee; flowers cost so much that I have to pick leaves, instead. We have cards for most foods. The only abundant shop windows are the drapers. Other shops parade tins, or cardboard boxes, doubtless empty . . . Suddenly one has come to notice the war everywhere.

Diary, 5 January 1918

I . . . went to Poland St. to get my watch. On the way I walked through a narrow street lined on both sides with barrows, where stockings & ironmongery & candles & fish were being sold. A barrel organ played in the middle. I bought 6 bundles of coloured tapers. The stir & colour & cheapness pleased me to the depths of my heart.

Diary, 8 April 1918

She had walked through the Berwick Street market, still one of the most cheerful sights in Soho.

By 1917 Zeppelin raids were frequent, especially at full moon; warnings and all-clears were sounded by bugles (sometimes blown by Boy Scouts).

The moon grows full, & the evening trains are packed with people leaving London. We saw the hole [caused by a German bomb three days before] in Piccadilly this afternoon. Traffic has been stopped, & the public slowly tramps past the place, which workmen are mending, though they look small in comparison with it. Swan & Edgar has every window covered with sacking or planks; you see shop women looking out from behind; not a glimpse of stuffs, but 'business goes on as usual' so they say. Windows are broken according to no rule; some intact, some this side, some that . . .

Diary, 22 October 1917

Nothing was further from our minds than air raids; a bitter night, no moon up till eleven. At 5 however I was wakened by L. to a most instant sense of guns: as if one's faculties jumped up fully dressed. We took clothes, quilts, a watch & a torch, the guns sounding nearer as we went down stairs to sit with the servants on the ancient black horse hair chest wrapped in quilts in the kitchen passage . . . Servants apparently calm & even jocose. In fact one talks through the noise, rather bored by having to talk at 5 a.m. than anything else. Guns at one point so loud that the whistle of the

shell going up followed the explosion . . . Then silence . . .
At last in the distance I heard bugles . . . it struck me how
sentimental the suggestion of the sound was, & how thousands of old ladies were offering up their thanksgiving at
the sound, & connecting him (a boy scout with small angel
wings) with some joyful vision . . .

Diary, 6 December 1917

*One evening she rode on the open top of a bus, from Oxford Street
to Victoria Station, at the moment when the sun set, the moon rose
and the searchlights began to play.*

I . . . observed how the passengers were watching the spec-
tacle: the same sense of interest & mute attention shown as
in the dress circle before some pageant. A Spring night;
blue sky with a smoke mist over the houses. The shops
were still lit; but not the lamps, so that there were bars of
light all down the streets; & in Bond Street I was at a loss to
account for a great chandelier of light at the end of the
street; but it proved to be several shop windows jutting out
into the road, with lights on different tiers. Then at Hyde
Park Corner the search light rays out, across the blue; part
of a pageant on a stage where all has been wonderfully
muted down. The gentleness of the scene was what impressed me.

Diary, 21 January 1918

*The Bloomsbury set had remained relatively immune to the war,
on pacifist or medical grounds, though one of Leonard Woolf's
brothers was killed in France. However, later that month nine
bombs fell on Kew, not far from the Woolfs' house at Richmond.
'You almost lost me,' Virginia wrote to her sister Vanessa, but she
added: 'I know raids dont interest you when no one you know is
killed.'*

Armistice

Letter to Vanessa Bell, 13 November 1918

. . . The rejoicing, so far as I've seen it, has been very sordid and depressing . . . A small boy was almost crushed in the tube at my feet; we were so packed we could hardly pick him out; everyone seemed half drunk – beer bottles were passed round – every wounded soldier was kissed, by women; nobody had any notion where to go or what to do; it poured steadily; crowds drifted up and down the pavements waving flags and jumping into omnibuses, but in such a disorganized, half hearted, sordid state that I felt more and more melancholy and hopeless of the human race. The London poor, half drunk and very sentimental or completely stolid with their hideous voices and clothes and bad teeth, make one doubt whether any decent life will ever be possible, or whether it matters if we're at war or at peace.

Post-war

Yesterday, Tuesday, I was treated to ices at Gunter's. It was all the same as before. Little tables; long rather dark shop; numbers of gilt chairs; discreet buffet; elderly waitresses in black; & couples scattered all about silently, or almost silently, absorbing ices & sugared cakes. There was an aristocratic small boy got up like a picture of Queen Victoria as a child, with a great sash, & a bow, & a hat wreathed in roses. His mother had brought him in, we thought, from one of the great Berkeley Street houses. Then there was youth, by some misadventure not at Ascot; a coffee-coloured young man, & a semi-transparent girl. We strolled out of this solemn cave & sauntered through the purest 18th Century London to the Green Park where we sat on hard green chairs, & watched people passing down the little slope towards the Palace.

Diary, 18 June 1919

Gunter's Tea Shop, founded in 1757, was on the east side of Berkeley Square, near the Hay Hill corner, and had always been famous for its ices – in earlier years generally eaten not inside the shop, but in the square outside. When the square was rebuilt in 1936 Gunter's moved to Curzon Street, behind the new Dorchester Hotel, and there I much enjoyed its nourishing artificial cream cakes during the next world war. It closed in 1956, having long outlived those 'great Berkeley Street houses'.

[London] is at the moment more repulsive than I can re-member. People have grown much more numerous and much uglier. Each time the door at the 1917 Club opens, a fresh deformity enters. I sit in a corner and stare in a kind of trance, as though one had fallen to the bottom of some awful pit in a nightmare. And they're all quite young – the coming generation – which makes it seem worse. In my youth, though crude, we were invariably lovely . . .

Letter to Lady Ottoline Morrell, mid-November 1919

The 1917 Club, in Gerard Street, Soho, was named after the February Revolution in Russia, and was a centre of radical thought much frequented by the Bloomsbury set.

In the winter of 1920 the remains of the Unknown Warrior were taken in solemn procession to Westminster Abbey in homage to all the dead of the Great War.

. . . Such a lurid scene, like one in Hell. A soundless street; no traffic; but people marching. Clear, cold & windless. A bright light in the Strand; women crying Remember the Glorious Dead, and holding out chrysanthemums. Always the sound of feet on the pavement. Faces bright and lurid . . . A ghastly procession of people in their sleep.

Diary, 12 December 1920

The Magic Carpet
Diary, 5 May 1924

London is enchanting. I step out upon a tawny coloured magic carpet, it seems, & get carried away into beauty without raising a finger. The nights are amazing, with all the white porticoes & broad silent avenues. And people pop in and out, lightly, divertingly like rabbits; & I look down Southampton Row, wet as a seal's back or red & yellow with sunshine, & watch the omnibus going & coming, & hear the old crazy organs. Faces passing lift up my mind; prevent it from settling . . .

'Really it is a disgrace,' wrote Virginia later that same year – 'the number of blank pages in this book! The effect of London on diaries is decidedly bad.'

Greenwich

. . . Pondered where shall I spend the day? decided on Greenwich, arrived there at 1; lunched; everything fell out pat; smoked a cigarette on the pier promenade, saw the ships swinging up, one two, three, out of the haze; adored it all; yes even the lavatory keepers little dog; saw the grey Wren buildings fronting the river; & then another great ship, grey & orange; with a woman walking on deck; & then to the hospital; first to the Museum where I saw Sir John Franklin's pen & spoons (a spoon asks a good deal of imagination to consecrate it) – I played with my mind watching what it would do, – & behold if I didn't almost burst into tears over the coat Nelson wore at Trafalgar with the medals which he hid with his hand when they carried him down, dying, lest the sailors might see it was him. There was too, his little fuzzy pigtail, of golden greyish hair tied in black; & his long white stockings, one much stained, & his white breeches with the gold buckles, & his stock – all of which I suppose they must have undone & taken off as he lay dying. Kiss me Hardy &c – Anchor, anchor, – I read it all when I came in, & could swear I was there on the Victory – So the charm worked in that case. Then it was raining a little, but I went into the Park, which is all prominence & radiating paths; then back on top of a bus, & so to tea.

Diary, 27 March 1926

Few ships now swing up to Greenwich, since the closing of the London docks on the opposite side of the river, and the Naval Museum that Virginia visited has now been closed. In 1926 it occupied part of the Royal Naval College, while Nelson's relics were in the college's marvellous Painted Hall, where his body lay in state after Trafalgar. Today it has been metamorphosed into the National Maritime Museum, in the Queen's House nearby, and there the Franklin and Nelson exhibits may still be seen. Greenwich Park, with its famous view and radiating paths, has been open to the public since the eighteenth century. I doubt if one could nowadays board a bus in Greenwich after lunch, a visit to the museum and a walk in the park, and be home in Bloomsbury for tea.

Nearly three years later Virginia Woolf went alone to Greenwich again – or was it the same visit re-enacted?

What an adventure! Think – I had lunch in a shop. Think – I sat on the pier and saw the ships bowling up. Women were walking on deck. Dogs looking out of portholes. The Captain on the Bridge. Never was anything so romantic and lovely. And then I wandered about the hospital, and saw Nelsons coat that he wore at Trafalgar, and his white stockings, and almost wept. What a day it was! How I shall remember it to the end of my life.

Letter to Vita Sackville-West, 8 January 1929

Scenes of the Great Depression, *1930s*

Last night we went to the gala opera ... Old women like Roman matrons, amply, tightly girt; girls wand like; many large clear stoned necklaces & long dresses. I got the feeling of this traditional English life; its garden like quality; flowers all in beds & rows; & the ceremony that has been in being so many years. Between the acts we all stood in the street; a dry brilliant night, with women all opening their cloaks: then came dribbling through us a draggled procession of poor women wheeling perambulators & carrying small, white haired dazed children; going across Waterloo Bridge. I watched Lady A's expression to see if she had children; but could only gather a momentary schoolboyish compunction. The women, involved in this garish feathered crowd, pushed on stolidly.

Diary, 24 June 1931

And last night we stopped the car in Hyde Park & I watched a people on the verge of ruin. How many Rolls Royces, & other low, pink, yellow, very powerful cars werent booming through the park like giant dor-beetles, with luxurious owners, men & women, lying back, on their way to some party. A Rolls Royce means £5000 a year. Then the children in perambulators with nurses. Then the strollers & saunterers. Then the mauve grey green trees, flushed with livid pinks & yellows; the may & the laburnum scarcely burning, like colour under water that cloudy, rainy, thunder yellow evening. So back through the West End – more cars blocked; & we on the verge of a precipice.

Diary, 4 June 1932

Nearly a quarter of Britain's insured workers were unemployed in mid-1931; by 1932 a coalition National Government was in power, so serious was the threat of economic collapse. The Rolls-Royce of 1931 was the Phantom II, to be had only with custom-built coachwork: with a Park Ward Sports Saloon body it sold for £2,425.

London Poetry
Letter to Ethel Smyth, 12 October 1934

I've been to Bromley and walked home across the Park. I'm too sleepy to tell you why I went to Bromley. But I like the London suburbs in autumn and their immense poetry. And I like Hyde Park fading into night, only the flowers burning in a few pale facades. I love overhearing scraps of talk by the Serpentine in the dusk; and thinking of my own youth, and wondering how far we live in other peoples and then buying half a pound of tea . . .

She had certainly not walked all the way from Bromley, an outer suburb in Kent; probably from Victoria Station by a roundabout route over Hyde Park to her house on Tavistock Square, in Bloomsbury.

To the Tower
Diary, 27 March 1935

Yesterday we went to the Tower, which is an impressive murderous bloody grey raven haunted military barrack prison dungeon place; like the prison of English splendour; the reformatory at the back of history; where we shot & tortured & imprisoned. Prisoners scratched their names, very beautifully, on the walls. And the crown jewels blazed, very tawdry, & there were the orders, like Spinks or a Regent St jewellers. And we watched the Scots Guards drill; & an officer doing a kind of tiger pace up & down – a wax faced barbers block officer trained to a certain impassive balancing. The sergeant major barked & swore. All in a hoarse bark: the men stamped & wheeled like – machines: then the officer also barked: all precise inhuman, showing off – a degrading, a stupifying sight, but in keeping with the grey wall the cobbles the executioner's block. People sitting on the river bank among old cannon. Ships &c. Very romantic: a dungeon like feeling.

The Death of a King, *1936*

The King [George V] died last night. We were dining with Alice Ritchie, & drove back past Buckingham Palace. It was a clear dry night, rather windy & rather cold. As we turned the corner & came by the Palace we saw cars drawn up all along the Mall. There were thin lights. On the white monument people were standing: only everybody seemed to be moving. There was a cluster like a swarm of bees, round the railings. Some people were plastered against the railings, holding on to the bars. There was a discreet frame, like a text, holding a bulletin. We had [to] drive on past the Monument before the policeman, who spoke with weary politeness, would let us stop. Then we got out, & walked back, crossing with difficulty because cars were passing all the time, & tried to shove our way through the crowd. But it was impossible. So I asked a policeman 'What is the latest bulletin?' And he said, It has not been issued. So I said But what is the latest news. I havent heard. (We had only seen Strength diminishing on the placards as we drove out) to which he replied 'His majesty's life is drawing to a peaceful close.' This he said without conviction, as if he were reciting words put into his mouth, but with a certain official tolerance. There was some agitation & excitement; many foreigners talking German; a large proportion of distinguished looking men, in semi evening dress; everyone indeed looked rather tall; but by no means tragic; yet not gay; rather suppressing their excitement; & it was all very brightly lit. As we turned away, a firework – a silver gilt sputtering fizzing torch began bubbling up, like a signal, like a festival, but it was presumably a photographers light. The crowd clustering on the rails became chalky white for a few seconds; & then we got into the car & drove home. The streets were very empty. But save for the occasional placard – it was now 'The King is Dying' – there was nothing out of the way. What I took for guns booming was only the banging of the loose door in the mews. But at 3 this morning, L. was woken by papers boys shouting in the street. The King had in fact died at 12.5. He was dead when we were outside the palace.

Diary, 21 January

The King might have lived for hours longer, allowing Leonard Woolf to sleep on, but his end had been hastened by a lethal injection from his doctor, Lord Dawson of Penn, partly to make his end more dignified, partly to make sure that the news would hit the morning press, rather than the 'less suitable' evening newspapers.

We stood in the Sqre to see the hearse: all London suddenly in an access of loyalty and democracy jumped the Sqre. railings, old greybearded ladies taking them at a flying leap, and though some stalwarts held the gates, the mob was on us, and Leonard who is a democrat was squashed between 5 fat grocers. This shows how enthusiastic Woburn Place was: and it all went by in 2 minutes, the crown glittering blue and white, and the long yellow leopards stretched over the coffin. In fact it was in its way, as they say, rather a magnificent, perfectly simple sight. Then there was a pause: then a vast royal omnibus in which sat an old woman carrying a parrots cage. How English!

Letter to Ethel Smyth, 23 January

Virginia reported in her diary that the King's last words had been 'How is the Empire?', but wags claimed he had really said 'What's on at the Empire?' (and there are alternative theories – see under 'Bognor' p. 64).

A King's Abdication
Diary, 10 December 1936

This is the first hour, or since it is 5.30, & the abdication [of Edward VIII] was announced at 4, the first hour & a half, of the new reign. Yes, I thought . . . I will go to Westminster. A bus took me to the top of Whitehall. There traffic was turned off & I dismounted. Whitehall was full of shuffling and trampling. People going both ways. Not a thick crowd – a moving crowd. A very beautiful yellow brown light: dry pavements: still lamps lit. Lines of light at Parliament Sqre. & the houses of Parliament in silhouette. The lamp burning in the watch tower. Opposite the Horse Guards there was Ottoline [Morrell], black, white, red lipped coming towards me . . . Has he abdicated? I asked. No, but they say he will. No one knew if he had or hadn't. A stir of uneasy feeling . . . most people half sad, yet also ashamed, yet also excited . . . Then on we wandered down the yellow brown avenue. We looked up at the beautiful carved front of – what office? I dont know. Thats the window out of which Charles the First stepped when he had his head cut off said Ottoline, pointing to the great lit up windows in their frame of white stone . . . I felt I was walking in the 17th century with one of the courtiers; & she was lamenting not the abdication of Edward – still though people shuffled this way & that – but the execution of Charles. Its dreadful, dreadful, she kept saying . . . Poor silly little boy – he always lost his temper. No one could ever tell him a thing he disliked. But to throw it away . . . Still he hadn't yet, so far as we knew, thrown it away. 'It' seemed then, looking at the curved street, & at the red & silver guards drawn up in the court-yard with the Park & the white government buildings behind, very stately, very lovely, very much the noble & severe aristocratic Stuart England . . . However, nothing seemed to happen. And she had a tea party: so we hailed a taxi. Have you any news? the man said. No. I dont know . . . What do you think? I say he should. We dont want a woman thats already had 2 husbands & an American when there [are] so many good English girls . . . We were thus driving & talking when a newspaper car drove by with the word Abdication very large on a placard. It stopped near us; & the first papers in the bale were bought by Ottoline & me.

Edward VIII had signed the Instrument of Abdication that morn-

ing, but the first hour of the new reign did not officially occur until the following day, when the Abdication Bill was passed by both Houses of Parliament, and Edward's brother the Duke of York became King George VI.

Two Walks in London, *1939*

Took the bus to Southwark Bridge. Walked along Thames Street; saw a flight of steps down to the river. I climbed down – a rope at the bottom. Found the strand of the Thames, under the warehouses – strewn with stones, bits of wire, slippery; ships lying off the [London] Bridge. Very slippery; warehouse walls crusted, weedy, worn. The river must cover them at high tide. It was now low. People on the Bridge stared. Difficult walking. A rat haunted, riverine place, great chains, wooden pillars, green slime, bricks corroded, a button hook thrown up by the tide. A bitter cold wind . . .

Diary, 31 January

Yesterday I went out in a fur coat, for it was bitter cold, to walk in London. I stopped by the Savoy Church: there were photographers. Soon the Bride arrived. The car glided on there were too many cars behind. Mother & small page arrived: 2 girls in absurd little boat hats. They helped the Bride with her veil. 'Can you get it over my bouquet?' she asked – very gay; rather red; very slim. Husband & best man waiting in grey trousers & cutaway coats. Old sitters in the sun watching. Camera men. A little procession – rather skimpy & cold & not very rich I thought. The old man – my age – had shabby boots. Shaven, brushed, red, thin. They are Mr Sholto Douglas Barnes, & Miss Marjorie Berkeley, daughter of a deceased ICS Colonel – so I learn today.

Diary, 29 April

In September 1940 the Woolfs drove to London from Sussex to find

Mecklenburgh Square, where their London house was, roped off after a night raid.

Wardens there, not allowed in. The house about 30 yards from ours struck at one this morning by a bomb. Completely ruined. Another bomb in the square still unexploded. We walked round the back. Stood by Jane Harrison's house. The house was still smouldering. That is a great pile of bricks. Underneath all the people who had gone down to their shelter. Scraps of cloth hanging to the bare walls at the side still standing. A looking glass I think swinging. Like a tooth knocked out – a clean cut . . . Who lived there? I suppose the casual young men & women I used to see, from my window; the flat dwellers who used to have flower pots & sit on the balcony. All now blown to bits – The garage man at the back – blear eyed & jerky told us he had been blown out of his bed by the explosion; made to take shelter in a church – a hard cold seat, he said, & a small boy lying in my arms. 'I cheered when the all clear sounded. I'm aching all over' . . .

Left the car & saw Holborn. A vast gap at the top of Chancery Lane. Smoking still. Some great shop entirely destroyed; the hotel opposite like a shell. In a wine shop there were no windows left. People standing at the tables – I think drink being served . . . So back to the car. A great block of traffic. The Cinema behind Mme Tussaud's torn open: the stage visible; some decoration swinging. All the R[egent's] Park houses with broken windows, but undamaged. And then miles & miles of orderly ordinary streets – all Bayswater, & Sussex Sqre as usual. Streets empty. Faces set & eyes bleared . . .

The people I think of now are the very grimy lodging house keepers, say in Heathcote Street; with another night to face: old wretched women standing at their doors; dirty, miserable.

Diary, 10 September 1940

London looked merry and hopeful, wearing her wounds like stars; why do I dramatize London perpetually? When I see a great smash like a crushed match box where an old house stood I wave my hand to London. What I'm finding odd and agreeable and unwonted is the admiration this war creates – for every sort of person: chars, shopkeepers, even much more remarkably, for politicians – Winston [Churchill] at least, and the tweed wearing sterling dull women here, with their grim good sense . . .

Letter to Ethel Smyth, 25 September 1940

The Woolfs' house had not been badly damaged in the raid of September 1940, but like two of Virginia's previous London homes, in Fitzroy Square and Tavistock Square, it was made uninhabitable. Thereafter they lived chiefly in Sussex, driving to London usually once a week for professional purposes. Virginia was never again to see London at peace, for she died in March 1941, long before the end of the war. By then the tone of voice she had adopted for Ethel Smyth (a general's daughter) had apparently entered her thinking too, and she could write of London, looking back upon her happy solitary walks there, that if a bomb destroyed one of the little City alleys with the brass-bound curtains and the river smell she would feel ' – well, what the patriots feel'.

London Pride

... The passion of my life, that is the City of London – to see London all blasted, that . . . raked my heart.

Letter to Ethel Smyth, 11 September 1940

... For Londoners, at any rate, there is only one real example of a town in the world – compared with her the rest are country villages.

Book review, **The Times Literary Supplement,** *9 November 1916*

Cornwall

London apart, it was the coast of England that Virginia Woolf loved the best. 'How anyone can live inland,' she wrote in 1909, 'I can't imagine; only clods and animals should be able to endure it.' Hills really existed, she thought, only to provide 'a wide view from them of the sea, the horizon, & one or two ships between . . . when you see nothing but land, stationary on all sides, you are conscious of being trapped, on a flat board'. The sea constituted a 'border of mystery, solving the limits of fields, and silencing their prose'. This preference doubtless arose from her lifelong love for the county of Cornwall. She first went there in the year of her birth, 1882, when her father took the lease of Talland House, St Ives (it belonged to the Great Western Railway Company) as a summer home. The family went there every year until 1894, and thereafter Virginia repeatedly returned to Cornwall on her own, with members of her family, or with her husband Leonard. 'My word,' she was still writing to Vita Sackville-West in 1936, 'what a country! Why do we ever spend any part of our short lives in Sussex Kent or London?' Her life as a writer, says Lyndall Gordon in her book Virginia Woolf: A Writer's Life, *was based upon two persistent sets of memories: those of her parents, and those of the north Cornwall shore. Her writings about Cornwall cover thirty years.*

Fin-de-siècle St Ives
From 'A Sketch of the Past', 1940

The town was then much as it must have been in the sixteenth century, unknown, unvisited, a scramble of granite
houses crusting the slope in the hollow under the Island . . .
It was a steep little town. Many houses had a flight of steps,
with a railing leading to the door. The walls were thick
blocks of granite built to stand the sea storms. They were
splashed with a wash the colour of Cornish cream. There
was nothing mellow about them; no red brick; no soft
thatch. The eighteenth century had left no mark upon St
Ives . . . It might have been built yesterday; or in the time of
the Conqueror. It had no architecture; no arrangement.
The market place was a jagged cobbled open place; the
Church was on one side, built of granite, ageless, like the
houses; the fish market stood beside it. There was no grass
in front of it. It stood flush to the market place. There were
no carved doors, large windows, no lintels; no moss; no
comely professional houses. It was a windy, noisy, fishy,
vociferous, narrow-streeted town; the colour of a mussel or
a limpet; like a bunch of rough shell fish clustered on a grey
wall together.

*Although St Ives is far from unknown or unvisited now, being one
of the most popular summer resorts in England, physically the
centre of the town, behind the peninsula known as the Island, is
still much as Virginia Woolf recalls it. Alleys are cobbled, houses
are whitewashed, and the streets behind the harbour are still
divided into the medieval quarters known as Downalong and
Upalong. Actually St Ives was not so unfrequented in the 1880s
and 1890s as Virginia Woolf remembered it, the coming of the
railway having opened it up to visitors from London. Well-known
artists were already working there, and high above the station,
behind Talland House, the railway company operated the large
and quite luxurious Tregenna Castle Hotel, where Henry James
stayed during a visit to the Stephens. It is still there.*

Going Back, *1905*

Eleven years after the Stephens family gave up the lease of Talland House, St Ives, Virginia, with her brothers and sister, returned to Cornwall for a nostalgic holiday.

It was with some feeling of enchantment that we took our places yesterday in the Great Western train. This was the wizard who was to transport us into another world, almost into another age. We would fain have believed that this little corner of England had slept under some enchanters spell since we last set eyes on it ten [eleven] years ago, & that no breath of change had stirred its leaves, or troubled its waters. There too, we should find our past preserved, as though through all this time it had been guarded & treasured for us to come back to one day — it mattered not how far distant. Many were the summers we had spent in St Ives; was it not reasonable to believe that as far away we cherished the memory of them, so here on the spot where we left them we should be able to recover something tangible of their substance?

It was dusk when we came, so that there still seemed to be a film between us & the reality. We could fancy that we were but coming home along the high road after some long day's outing, & that when we reached the gate at Talland House, we should thrust it open, & find ourselves among the familiar sights again. In the dark, indeed, we made bold to humour this fancy of ours further than we had a right to; we passed through the gate, groped stealthily but with sure feet up the carriage drive, mounted the little flight of rough steps, & peered through a chink in the escalonia hedge. There was the house, with its two lighted windows; there on the terrace were the stone urns, against the bank of tall flowers; all, so far as we could see was as though we had but left it in the morning. But yet, as we knew well, we could go no further; if we advanced the spell was broken. The lights were not our lights; the voices were the voices of strangers. We hung there like ghosts in the shade of the hedge, & at the sound of footsteps we turned away.

From the raised platform of the high road we beheld the curve wh. seemed to enclose a great sweep of bay full tonight of liquid mist, set with silver stars & we traced the promontory of the island, & saw the cluster of lights which nestle in its warm hollow.

The dawn however rose upon that dim twilight & showed us a country of bright hill sides, of cliffs tumbling in a cascade of brown rocks into the sea, &, alas, we saw also not a few solid white mansions where the heather used to spring. They have cut a broad public road too, where we stumbled along a foot path on the side of the moor, & there are signs . . . that the whole place has been tidied up since our day. There are differences though, which only strike a very fresh eye, & in two days time we see only the permanent outlines of the moor & island, & the place is in substance & detail unchanged.

Diary, 11 August

One may still travel by train to St Ives on British Rail's Western Region, successor to the GWR – by the InterCity express from London as far as St Erith, and then on a single-track line along the coast to St Ives. Talland House, which stands on a hill to the east of the town centre, above St Ives Bay, is now divided into holiday flats, but still possesses part of the garden that Virginia peered into; across the road is the Porthminster Hotel which, when it went up in 1893, so damaged the view that the Woolfs decided to give up the house. The view itself was to be fictionally immortalised in To the Lighthouse, 1927: ' . . . *the great plateful of blue water . . . the hoary Lighthouse, distant, austere, in the midst; and on the right, as far as the eye could see, fading and falling, in soft low pleats, the green sand dunes with the wild flowing grasses on them, which always seemed to be running away into some moon country . . . '*

Today we did what we have long promised ourselves to do on the first opportunity, that is we hired a fishing boat & went for a sail in the bay. But the sea was so calm that great stretches of it had a dull surface, & our sail made no attempt to lift the boat. Our boatman, had to take his oars, & for amusement we lay back & watched the tawny sail flapping against the sky, & tried to make the man discourse of the sea. He was induced to tell us how, last winter, he had been capsized in his herring boat; how he had been rescued as by a miracle, as he clung to the keel; how he would be off on the same toil next month, & how he would make one of the crew of the seine boats which lie waiting for pilchards in the bay. At this moment the monotony of our slow progress was relieved by a sudden exclamation of porpoises; & not far distant we saw a shiny black fin performing what looked like a series of marine cartwheels.

We sailed into the midst of a whole school of these gymnasts who came so near that we could hear their gulp for breath before they dived again.

Diary, 14 August

Porpoises still sometimes appear in St Ives Bay. The image of the 'shiny black fin' was to haunt Virginia. It entered her mind often at moments of great stress or anxiety, and played an imaginative part in the gestation of her novel The Waves: *'I have netted that fin in the waste of waters,' she wrote when she finished the book, and was sitting 'in a state of glory, & calm, & some tears'. An earlier boat trip had provided the theme of* To the Lighthouse, *for in 1892 Virginia had sailed to the Godrevy light with her elder brother Thoby, while her younger brother Adrian was upset at not being allowed to go – a memory which became one of the novel's motifs.*

I thought today on my solitary walk on the scarcity of good roads in Cornwall. In the South you find it difficult to escape from the road; broad & smoothly hammered they drive across the country at all angles. Even the lesser paths are workmanlike & strike directly at their destination. We have here our High Road, which however bears such marks of rusticity that it would be accounted a lane elsewhere. Once you step aside you must trust innumerable little footpaths, as thin as though trodden by rabbits, which lead over hills & through fields in all directions. The Cornish substitute for a gate is simple; in building a wall of granite blocks they let two or three jut out at convenient intervals so as to form steps; you often find these arranged beside a gate which is heavily padlocked, as though the farmer winked one eye at the trespasser. The system of course has its advantages for the native, or for one well acquainted with the lie of the country; it keeps the land fluid, as it were, so that the feet may trace new paths in it at their will; but the stranger must often prefer the cut & dry system of regular high roads.

The secondary roads, moreover, are not only badly preserved, but sometimes after starting out bravely enough they dwindle off into a track across the heather. The pedestrian then should sketch his path with a free hand, & trust that he will find some little trodden line to guide him; for in the course of an afternoon's tramp he need not strike the road.

There are very few villages in this country, & the little clusters of gray farms which gather among the hills connect themselves with the main road by some roughly worked roadway of their own, leading directly into the farm yard. A traveller who follows the track finds herself at the end of half a mile or so confronted by a lean sheep dog, & a sour looking farmer's wife who is scouring the milk pails & resents the intrusion. But for the walker who prefers the variety & incident of the open fields to the orthodox precision of the high road, there is no such ground for walking as this.

Diary, August (undated)

It was more, perhaps, to fulfil a tradition than for the sake of any actual pleasure that we took the train into St Ives this afternoon, the day of the Regatta. I, it must be confessed, secretly expected some present & not merely retrospective enjoyment from the crowd, the gay flags, & the fitful trumpets of the band. This was the scene I remembered; vaguely joyful & festive, without reference to the swimming or the sailing which we pretended to watch. I remembered the crowd of little boats, the floating flags along the course, & the Committee boat, dressed with lines of bunting, from which naked figures plunged, & guns were fired. A certain distant roll of drums & blare of trumpets, we confessed to each other, never fails where ever we hear it to suggest St Ives Regatta day on such [a] bright afternoon as this ... The band was playing on the Malakoff, now as then; on close inspection we saw that a venerable clergyman waved the conductor's staff, although the music that issued from his beat was certainly secular in type. Two or three little booths for the sale of sweets & cakes lined the terrace, & the whole population of St Ives paraded up & down in their reds & greens.

There was the Committee boat, & the little rowing boats, the flags on the water, & the swimmers poised for a moment before the gun sent them shooting into the sea, & the general stir of talk & movement. Reduce it all to a French impressionist picture & the St Ives Regatta is not a sight to be despised.

Diary, August (undated)

The Malakoff is a former redoubt, named after a fortress made famous during the Siege of Sevastopol in the Crimean War, which overlooks St Ives Bay and has long been used as a public promenade. Now heavily prettied up by the municipality, it contains a statue by Barbara Hepworth (1903-75), who lived and worked in St Ives.

We make expeditions, it seems to me, more for the sake of the going & the coming & the delicious meal in the open air, than because there is any special sight of beauty to be found in the spot where we pitch our resting place. I have found, on my walks here a dozen places as I think to which one might fitly go on pilgrimages, but they are sudden, un-expected, secret; no one, perhaps, will step that way for weeks, or will see precisely what I saw for months, or even years. Those are the sights which surprise the solitary walker & linger in the memory. So, as these little visions are not to be evoked at will by any combination of steam & horse, it is safer to fix upon certain recognised spots & to make them the goal of any expedition you choose to undertake.

Such a goal is the Lands End, where the imagination at any rate is infallibly impressed, & one is tolerably sure to find more substantial beauties for the eye. Unfortunately, the pitch of green turf, with the craggy rocks on it, the cliffs, & the romantic line of coast are the property nowadays of a hundred eyes; every ten minutes or so a lumbering brake or a dusty motor car deposits its load of sight seers upon this little stretch of land.

But though the spot itself is thus made hideous, the land all round is still lonely & very beautiful. On the rim of the horizon the eye may see some rock shaped shadow to which, as the sun sank & made it golden, we gave the name of the Fortunate Isles. When Cornwall was chill in the shade, there was bright daylight over there – perhaps per-petual afternoon.

Diary, August (undated)

Virginia would not be greatly pleased, I fear, by the Land's End theme park, which now occupies the tip of the peninsula. It attracts more cars than she could ever have imagined, and it in-cludes as its centrepiece The Legendary Last Labyrinth, a Multi-Sensory Experience that Defies the Everyday Limits of Time and Space.

It is a great thing in this little lodging house that we look on the sea from all the large windows. When I wake in the morning I discover first what new ships have come in to the bay, all day long these silent voyagers are coming & going, alighting like some travelling birds for a moment & then shaking out their sails again & passing on to new waters. Where do they come from, & whither are they bound? A ship moves in mysterious ways. In the morning we see the luggers starting for their fishing grounds; late in the afternoon they come racing back on the wind, like so many birds swooping on their prey. Most beautiful of all are the great sailing ships, which ply up & down the Channel.

Diary, August (undated)

The 'little lodging house' was at Carbis Bay, along the road from St Ives, which was a fishing village then, but is now a sprawling seaside suburb. Few fishing boats work out of St Ives nowadays, but small ships often come into the bay to shelter in bad weather, and out at sea the Channel traffic still passes. The most striking vessels to be seen nowadays are towering oil rigs, being towed to or from the shipyards at Falmouth.

It is a mistake to keep rigidly to the coast; strike inland & cross the hills, & then you will sight a broad ribbon of sea beneath you, & ships set like toys about it. The land has been draped in all kinds of strange folds at the edge, so that instead of a sheer cliff you find beautiful little valleys with triangular beaches at the bottom of them. Here we spread our tea, & that finished, walk home again in the dark. Last night it was dusk when we started, but we had to take a long look at the Gurnard's Head & the misty shapes beyond, through which suddenly there flashed the fitful glare of the St Just lighthouse. It was late then when we turned back, & we resolved to keep safe upon the road. Before that could be reached we had to fight our way through a forest of ferns which bound ones legs together & brought one to ones knees. The road when we reached it was of a vague white mist upon which our feet struck hard, even to our surprise. A.s [Adrian, her younger brother] figure stalking ahead was blurred & without outline, & at a hundreds yards distance we had to send our voices out after him to make sure that we had not lost him. In this mystification we left the road, & stepped into a vast trackless country, without mark or boundary. Before us dozens of lights were scattered, floating in soft depths of darkness without anchorage on the firm ground. A. trod on unswervingly, clearing aside the mists as though the road lay bright before him. Once in this strange pilgrimage we groped our way through a farm-yard, where the shapes of dim cattle loomed large, & a great lantern swung an unsteady disk of light across our faces. The voice of the farmer bidding us good night recalled us for a moment to the cheerful land of substance, but our path lay on into the darkness again. We stumbled across fields which swam in dusky vapours; we struck the road, & suddenly a great light shone in front of us, & a cart wheel crunched the ground just beyond us as though the sound of its approach had been muffled in the night. Now we had come to the lights in the valley, & we passed lighted windows, scarcely able to irradiate a yard of the blackness that pressed on them, & could just discover long black figures leaning against the walls quiescent. Night was weighing heavily on this little village; all was silent though not asleep. Then we went on, up to the top of a hill, & again beneath us we saw those great swarms of lights which spring up in the dark where by day there is nothing. And so once more we found the road again, & the familiar lamps of homes. But how narrow were those walls, & how intense that light after the vague immensity of the air; we were like creatures lately winged that have been caught & caged.

Diary, August (undated)

Suddenly T. [Thoby, her older brother] threw up the window & shouted 'pilchards in the bay'.

We leapt as though we were in the seine boat ourselves, & before half past nine we were out by the Hewers house on the point. It was at once obvious that the news was more than true. Not only were there pilchards but two nets were already out, lying like dark scars in the water in the bay. The gathering of the Hewers was not large as yet, but it was eminently professional. A line of watchers stood on the wall all the way along: some with megaphones, others with globes tied up in white bags. Great was the excitement for the schools of fish were still passing through the bay & all the pilchard boats were in motion like long black insects with rows of legs. Our friend Mr. Hain called us to him & showed us a certain faint purple shadow, passing slowly outside the rocks. That was a shoal he said – the boats were coming round to shoot their seines over it. As they neared the place the megaphones brayed unintelligibly & the white globes were waved emphatically. Answering shouts came from the boats. Finally we saw that two boats had stopped & the rowers were picking up handfuls of net & dropping them over board; as they did this they slowly separated, & made the dotted line of the net spread out in a circle between them; all the time the shouts went on, for the men at the hewers were guiding every movement; they alone could tell the exact position of the fish. The net was then joined & the boat went through various manoeuvres with the low ropes. It was just possible for us now that it was thus circumscribed to see the faint spin of deeper purple within the circle; it looked like one of those sudden ruffles of shade which pass across the sea like blushes.

The crowd was now gathering, & we walked from one point to another vainly trying to interpret the hoarse commands of the megaphone which might, for all we understood of them, have been in Cornish. Mr. Hain came running down again, after a time with the news that another school was sighted round the head land; the boats were not yet on the spot. At the Hewers house an intense excitement prevailed. The shoal having rounded the point was the property apparently of the Carbis Bay boats, which had hitherto remained at anchor. They were now underway, & the Hewer who directed them had clambered on to the roof of the Hewers house to make directions more forcible. The boats came slowly towards the floating shadow which we thought we could detect beyond the Carrack rocks. As they neared it, the megaphones roared like foghorns. A certain dwarf in particular had leapt to the roof & was brandishing the white globes as though they were dumb-bells. The boats began to drop the seine; they had half completed the circle when a storm of abuse broke from the hewers house. Language such as I will not try to reproduce swore at them for a boatload of incompetent monkeys; the school was further to the westward & not a fish would enter the nets. 'To the west, west, west,' roared the megaphones & the naked voices took up the word in the agony of excitement. But pilchard boats are unwieldy things, & their motion was slow. The Hewers could actually see the fish slipping past the point & the net cast in empty water. A thousand pounds as we afterwards learnt, was floating out of their reach. No wonder that the excitement was painful. The net finally enclosed a small portion of the school, & the rest fell a prey to the rival boats. Four seines were now shot & we thought it time to take a boat to the first of them which had been slowly drawn close in to shore. We therefore walked round to the harbour & were rowed out to the spot. When we came near we saw that the enclosed school was of a deep & unmistakable purple; little spurts of water were flickering over the surface, & a silver flash leapt into the air for a second. We took up our places by the row of corks & waited; after a time the empty pilchard boats with their baskets drew up & let down a smaller net, called the tucking net, in the centre of the larger one, so that all the fish were gathered in a small compass. Now all the boats made a circle round the inner net, & the two boats who held the net gradually drew it up. The water within seethed with fish. It was packed with iridescent fish, gleaming silver & purple, leaping in the air, lashing their tails, sending up showers of scales.

Then the baskets were lowered & the silver was scooped up & flung into the boats; it was a sight unlike any one has seen elsewhere, hardly to be described or believed. The fishermen shouted & the fish splashed. The baskets were filled, emptied & plunged into the bubbling mass again, again & again. Nothing seemed to lessen the quantities. The little boats took their fill of fish as they liked; the fishermen stopped to pelt the onlookers with fish; the wealth was inexhaustible.

Diary, August (undated)

St Ives was nearing the end of its history as one of Britain's chief pilchard ports. In 1868, 16 million fish had been caught in a single seine net off the town, but by 1905 the catches had been greatly reduced, and within a few years the industry would collapse. The Hewers' house, not far along the sea-bluff from Talland House, was the fishermen's watch-post, and is still there. It supposedly takes its name from the Cornish-language cry of the watchmen, 'Heva!', perhaps meaning a hunt (cf. hemolc'h *in Breton), or perhaps, as a Breton sceptic suggests to me, simply 'Hooray!' Cornish, which was closely akin to Breton, had been in a spectral condition since the beginning of the nineteenth century, and had not yet begun its current revival – only a very few enthusiasts could speak it in 1905.*

Christmas in Cornwall
Letter to Clive Bell, 26 December 1909

It is past nine o'clock, and the people still sing carols beneath my window [at the Lelant Hotel, in Lelant], which is open, owing to the clemency of the night. I am at the crossroads, and at the centre of the gossip of the village. The young men spend most of the day leaning against the wall, and sometimes spitting. Innumerable hymns and carols issue from barns and doorsteps. Several windows, behind which matrons sit, are red and yellow, and a number of couples are wandering up and down the roads, which shine dimly. Then there is the [Godrevy] lighthouse, seen as through steamy glass, and a grey flat where the sea is. There is no moon, or stars, but the air is soft as down, and one can see trees on the ridge of the road, and the shapes of everything without any detail. No one seems to have any wish to go to bed. They circle aimlessly. Is this going on in all the villages of England now?

It is a busy main road that the Lelant Hotel, now renamed the Badger, today overlooks. Opposite stands a memorial to the local men killed in the two world wars since 1909, some of them doubtless among those who lounged and spat at the crossroads. I am assured that from no bedroom in the hotel can the Godrevy light be seen.

Going Back Again, *1921*

In the spring of 1921 Virginia and Leonard spent a holiday at Ponion, near Zennor, on the coast below St Ives. It was no more than a hamlet above the sea, and their landlady, Mrs Hosking, belonged to a family well known in the area to this day.

Here we are on the verge of going to Cornwall. This time tomorrow – it is now 5.20 – we shall be stepping on to the platform at Penzance, sniffing the air, looking for our trap, & then – Good God! – driving off across the moors to Zennor – Why am I so incredibly & incurably romantic about Cornwall? One's past, I suppose: I see children running in the garden. A spring day. Life so new. People so enchanting. The sound of the sea at night. And now I go back 'bringing my sheaves' – well, Leonard, & almost 40 years of life, all built on that, permeated by that: how much so I could never explain. And in reality it is very beautiful. I shall go down to Treveal & look at the sea – old waves that have been breaking precisely so these thousand years.

Diary, 22 March 1921

It is pitiable to think that you are bothering about pictures and no doubt losing your umbrella on Haverstock Hill while I am watching two seals barking in the sea at Gurnards Head. This is no poetic licence. There they were, with their beautifully split tails, and dog shaped heads, rolling over and diving like two naked dark brown old gentlemen. Two minutes before a viper started up under my feet. The smell of the gorse which is all in bloom and precisely like a Cornish picture against a purple sea is like – I dont really know what. Then there are deep rivers running down with all those plants that used to grow in Halsetown bog.

We are on the cliff, quite by ourselves, nothing but gorse between us and the sea, and when I have done this letter we are going to take our books and roll up in a hollow over the sea, and there watch the spray and the ships and the bees . . .

Letter to Vanessa Bell, 27 March 1921

The house they rented is still there, still with nothing but gorse between it and the sea, and with a small stream running down a gulley beside it. Two houses alongside make up the rest of Ponion, and behind, across the St Ives road, are the bare moors.

Next holiday you must come here. Mrs Hosking is quite adequate, though suffering from the death of her husband, which has affected her eyes, and thus a little irresponsive to my endearments, but speaking – as they all do – a faultless and colourless English. But the country – my dear Saxon. We are between Gurnards Head and Zennor: I see the nose of the Gurnard from my window. We step out into the June sunshine, past mounds of newly sprung gorse, bright yellow and smelling of nuts, over a grey stone wall, so along a cart track scattered with granite to a cliff, beneath which is the sea, of the consistency of innumerable plovers eggs where they turn grey green semi transparent. However when the waves curl over they are more like emeralds, and then the spray at the top is blown back like a mane – an old simile doubtless, but rather a good one. Here we lie roasting, though L. pretends to write an article for the Encyclopaedia upon Cooperation. The truth is we can't do anything but watch the sea – especially as the seals may bob up, first looking like logs, then like naked old men, with tridents for tails. I'm not sure though that the beauty of the country isn't its granite hills, and walls, and houses, and not its sea. What do you say? Of course its very pleasant to come upon the sea spread out at the bottom, blue, with purple stains on it, and here a sailing ship, there a red steamer. But last night walking through Zennor the granite was – amazing, is the only thing to say I suppose, half transparent, with the green hill behind it, and the granite road curving up and up. All the village dogs were waiting outside the church, and the strange Cornish singing inside, so unlike the English.

I think a good deal about the Phoenicians and the Druids . . .

Letter to Saxon Sydney-Turner, 28 March 1921

By looking over my left shoulder I see gorse yellow against the Atlantic blue, running up, a little ruffled, to the sky, today hazy blue. And we've been lying on the Gurnard's Head, on beds of samphire among grey rocks with buttons of yellow lichen on them. How can I pick out the scene? You look down on to the semi-transparent water – the waves all scrambled into white round the rocks – gulls swaying on bits of seaweed – rocks now dry now drenched with white waterfalls pouring down crevices. No one near us, but a coastguard sitting outside the house.

We took a rabbit path round the cliff, & I find myself a little shakier than I used to be. Still however maintaining without force to my conscience that this is the loveliest place in the world. It is so lonely. Occasionally a very small field is being ploughed, the men steering the plough round the grey granite rocks. But the hills & the cliffs have been given over as a bad job. There they lie graceful even in spite of all their stones & roughness, long limbed, stretching out to sea; & so subtly tinted; greys, all various with gleams in them; getting transparent at dusk; & soft grass greens; & then one night they burnt the heather at Tregerthen, the smoke rolling up over the crest, & flame shining . . . The Eagle's Nest stands up too much of a castle-boardinghouse to be a pleasant object; but considering the winds, firm roots are needed. Endless varieties of nice elderly men to be seen there, come for climbing.

Diary, 30 March 1921

The Eagle's Nest, a couple of miles along the road from Ponion, was a large house belonging to Virginia's friends the Arnold-Forster family. It is still the chief landmark of the district, and has long been the home of the artist Patrick Heron. The best rock-climbing in those parts is on the neighbouring sea-cliffs.

The Last Visit
Letter to Vita Sackville-West, 14 May 1936

What a country! . . . We dribble from bay to bay, and have discovered an entirely lonely country – not a bungalow – only gulls foot prints on sand. Here and there a castle, and an old man fishing in his river with the sea breaking behind ilex groves, and a rim of green hill.

Virginia Woolf never went to Cornwall again. She might not recognise the 'entirely lonely country' today.

Sussex

Virginia Woolf had a long association with Sussex, and after 1910, when she rented a house at Firle, near Lewes, her links with the eastern half of the county were unbroken until her death. From 1912 until 1919 she rented Asham (or Asheham) House at Beddingham, not far away, and her sister Vanessa came to live close by at Charleston. Finally in 1919 Virginia and Leonard Woolf bought, for £700, Monk's House at Rodmell, which was to be her country home for the rest of her life. She adored, she said, the 'emptiness, bareness, air & colour' of the country – 'a relic I think of my fathers feeling for the Alps'.

Bognor, 1897

Virginia Woolf's first experience of Sussex occurred in the winter of 1897, when she accompanied her sister Vanessa, her half-sister Stella and Stella's future husband Jack Hills, who was convalescing from an operation, on a week's holiday in Bognor (now Bognor Regis). They took lodgings on the seafront. Leslie Stephen came down from London to visit them, and Virginia detested every moment of it.

We are the end house of the [Cottesmore] Crescent, which

has never been finished . . . very dismal and cold – looking out on to the sea which is a black and rather inferior sea. Bicycled with Nessa once up and down the 'Esplanade', but it was too windy and cold for more.

Diary, 8 February

Cottesmore Crescent, unfinished in 1897, has now vanished: mercifully, perhaps.

Walked in the morning on the sands – Very dull and grey and windy and cold . . . It was too windy to bicycle, and altogether very dismal – We are the only people here, apparently; except 3 or 4 girls schools, which parade up and down outside in the rain – Two bath chairs have also been discovered.

Diary, 9 February

After lunch we all walked along the Pier, which is very long, and very very dull. Two ladies out fishing but otherwise no one else there at all . . . Came home over the fields, which are perfectly flat, and covered with thick clay into which you sink at every step. The drizzle developed into rain before we were half way home, and we splashed along in the mud and wet, umbrellaless, most dismally – 'Never saw such an ugly country and such bad weather in my life' is fathers remark – to which I agree.

Diary, 10 February

We settled to go to Arundel in the afternoon by the 2.25, to see the Castle. We just missed the train, and had to hire a fly – the fly was dragged by a most broken down old horse, all ribs and knock knees. It is 9 miles to Arundel, through very flat uninteresting country – great brown ploughed fields, and ditches and miserable wind blown trees – through this we were drawn first at a trot, which became slower and slower till the creature merely walked . . . After a spirt of two minutes, the horse stopped, and refused to move – We got out and walked – The castle shut up and being repaired.

Diary, 12 February

A proposal that they should spend another week in Bognor was fortunately aborted, Virginia 'absolutely refusing' to stay, so despite their landlady's protestations that such fearful weather had never been seen in Bognor before, they 'marched to the station' and returned to London.

Thank Goodness! Another week of drizzle in that muddy flat utterly stupid Bognor (the very name suits it) would have drive me to the end of the pier and into the dirty yellow sea beneath.

Diary, 13 February

Virginia could not have foreseen the alleged last words of George V, from whom the place later took its 'Regis'. The King was assured that he would soon be well enough to return to his beloved Bognor, where he had convalesced in 1929. 'Bugger Bognor', he is supposed to have replied.

A Visit to Rye, *1907*

In 1907 Virginia and her brother Adrian took The Steps, a house at Playden, outside Rye, for a summer holiday.

Last night, as it was fine as gauze, we speculated a little from our terrace, & heard the faint blare of drums & trumpet. A fair? we asked; & set off, for the sake of the walk, & perhaps some happy accident of light & rustic comedy, to follow the sound. We went down to Rye by the road; & met a number of silent passengers, driving or walking, though it was close upon eleven; which gave one an odd notion of the populousness of the country, & all the odd businesses that these people must be following. In Rye itself there was much pale light of street lamps, some lounging figures, but no fair to be seen, band to be heard. We walked back then, by way of the road skirting the marsh, which leads beneath our cliff. The flats glistened beneath the moon, & there were odd smooth barns by the wayside, all dark, like colour shapes in some 18th century water colour. Sportsmen might shoot snipe here in daylight, in long coats; by night there would be the poacher or the highwayman, or the great London coach, baiting its horses at the turn, or paying toll. When we stood silent, a little harmony of noises crowded upon our ears. The dogs bark of course, then the cough of certain sheep, out in the fields, then the cry of some bird. At last a great luminous train, semi transparent, came rattling before us; with a body like some phosphorescent caterpillar, & a curled plume of smoke, all opal & white, issuing from the front of it. Then there was a very dark land with bright bars of moon light across it, so white that our shadows were cut in them. And then our frail little house, which we manage to think so substantial, with its eye of light, like many others; no, we don't include the world here. We are dotted about on the surface & exclude an infinite number of things.

Diary, 22 August

The wish to write down some picture of what is now going on here, in the county of Sussex, in the month of September, really vexes me, when ever I take a walk. Yesterday for example we all started along the road to Winchelsea, in a colourless eventide which soon became of a drifting grey tint as the clouds trailed along the wind & sprayed our faces. Winchelsea on its sombre mound grew almost ink black, with those deep liquid shadows (as though composed of many different grades of blackness): there was light towards Rye, but the highest point was the barrel of the windmill, which was gray. The clouds shift, drag apart, & go in tattered sheets hanging down with frayed edges right across the landscape; filling all the air with different lights & glooms, populating it, giving it variety & romance. Our best view is that we take from the hill top here; you see Rye pointed with lights, sombrely massed upon its hill; dark tonight as though the rain had drowned some of those fine points so star clear on other nights. And the land all round was black & turbulent as the sea; while we could still see the clouds changing & travelling in the air; only it seemed as though the air itself was all broken & confused, a shattered medium, no longer a tranquil void for clouds to sail in. The river lay quite pale at the base of the hill; the clearest & most peaceful thing in the landscape.

There is a certain evening hour, when the tides meet I think it is, when walking is the finest treat; even on a chill day such as this. The road is but a blurred grey vapour – & people & things come towards you all distorted & unfamiliar; walking too at a strange quick pace, upon you & past you before you expect it. The light of a carriage lamp cast on the hedge has the effect of some spectral shrouded figure, just about to taper into a point & disappear. Happy ecstasies float the mind out into the vague; spur it & seek not to recall it.

Diary, 3 September

It is beautiful at evening to walk out along the bed of the sea – now all slippery hay coloured grass, with curving dykes, to Camber Castle, the grey trefoil which lies midway between Rye & Winchelsea. The grey of this old stone fuses the landscape, if, writing in haste & in private, I may so outrage – is it sense or sound? – All the view that is has a lovely pallor – whites & silver greens – pale straw colour; the pearl white sheep make the highest light in the landscape; & always on either side there are the two shaded bones of Rye & Winchelsea; Rye; it is true, still bristling with red roofs & chimneys, but Winchelsea all sunk into the dark layers of its foliage. In the background – if we walk upon a stage as it seems, with our faces to the audience of the sea, there are the softly flowing hills, & there behind Winchelsea a high screen of down, with an oblong church on the top of it. It is a view full of charm of a certain transparent lucidity; a little shallow, as though you could see through the tints if the light were just a trifle stronger; but at sunset the depth is exactly right, & luminous.

Diary, 3 September

Let me note the effect at Camber Castle tonight of the grey stone walls against a sky of scarlet plumes. The stones seemed as though blurred, with a rough surface, & the colour was more muffled than usual; with a suffusion of violet tint in it. The ring of castle wall holds in the heat, like a cup brimming with soft vapours.

The grass also within the circle is far softer, & richer, more of the nature of garden turf than the coarse sea-salt grass marsh land outside.

The chimneys of the town, rising in steps, make the outline, at a distance, of the little pyramid, bristle. All might still compress itself as though for safety, within the girdle of one wall; you see, from the East, tall lodging houses leaning back, with their sides all ablaze with sheets of glass.

Diary, 3 September

There is a little angle, in the town wall, a ledge with a seat running along it – a railing to save one from the precipice, where the natives of Rye nightly observe the sunset. The sun sets just behind Winchelsea, staining all that steep space of air & chequering the marsh land with liquid yellows, & mellow shadows, before blotting it out once again for another night. The mounds, or cliffs, – you cant call them hills, so sudden & unexpected are they, solidify as evening draws on, & make great soft blots on the landscape, otherwise so wide & simple. And then the sea is still there to the South, hoarding the last blue, & still going about its business, carrying ruddy fishing boats, & all the busy craft of steamers. Now there is a pale yellow light, opening & shutting as some single eye, & a breeze drives the old creatures who are drinking their last dose of sunlight, to shelter. Will they have a lamp, & read some pious gross old book? or the letter from some daughter in service? You meet the same people night after night.

Diary, 3 September

The Steps in Playden is a charming house (Virginia thought it rather too *charming) down a well-wooded cul-de-sac off the road to Rye, and was quite new in 1907. During her stay there Virginia Woolf went to tea with Henry James at his house in Rye, and learnt from him the local scandal – 'Mr Jones has eloped, I regret to say, to Tasmania . . . most regrettable, most unfortunate, and yet not wholly an action to which one has no private key of ones own so to speak . . . ' Virginia's visit is still well remembered at The Steps, and when I called there in 1992 I was encouraged to meditate on the terrace from which, so long before, she and Adrian had heard the illusory trumpets.*

War and Peace in East Sussex

During both world wars, and during the peacetime years be-tween, Virginia Woolf spent much of her time at her homes in east Sussex. She loved the landscapes there, and was constantly agi-tated by threats of developments real or hypothetical. Although she never wrote lengthy descriptive passages about the countryside, especially in the 1930s her letters and diaries were sprinkled with snatches of evocation.

Oh I'm so flea-bitten! – no, its harvesters, the result of the most divinely lovely walk through stubble this after-noon. I found the loneliest of valleys with silver sheep clustering on the sides, hares leaping from my foot, and, great horses slowly dragging wagons like shaggy sea monsters – but corn was dripping instead of sea weed . . . My word, when one shuts off the villas, this land is I think the fairest far in all Arabia.

Letter to Ethel Smyth, 15 September 1932

Oh its so lovely on the downs now – a dewpond like a silver plate in the hollow; and all the hills, not distinct as in summer, but vast, smooth, shaven, serene; and I lie on the ground and look; and then the bells tinkle, and then the horses plough . . .

Letter to Ethel Smyth, 28 December ('or thereabouts') 1932

It has been almost beyond belief here – I walk and walk by the river on the downs in a dream, like a bee, or a red admiral, quivering on brambles, on haystacks; and shut out the cement works and the villas. Even they melted in the yellow light have their glory.

Letter to Lady Ottoline Morrell, 7 October 1933

We are at Rodmell on the loveliest spring day: soft: a blue veil in the air torn by birds voices. I am glad to be alive & sorry for the dead . . .

Diary, 24 March 1932

At the height of the First World War, when Virginia was living at Asham, from the South Downs above she could easily hear the guns of the battles being fought in France.

. . . It sounds like the beating of gigantic carpets by gigantic women, at a distance. You may almost see them holding the carpets in their strong arms by the four corners, tossing them into the air, and bringing them down with a thud while the dust rises in a cloud about their heads. All walks on the Downs this summer are accompanied by this sinister sound of far-off beating, which is sometimes as faint as the ghost of an echo, and sometimes rises almost from the next fold of grey land. At all times strange volumes of sound roll across the bare uplands, and reverberate in those hollows in the Downside which seem to await the spectators of some Titanic drama. Often walking alone, with neither man nor animal in sight, you turn sharply to see who it is that gallops behind you. But there is no one. The phantom horseman dashed by with a thunder of hoofs, and suddenly his ride is over and the sound lapses, and you only hear the grasshoppers and the larks in the sky.

Such tricks of sound may easily be accounted for by the curious planes of curve and smoothness into which these Downs have been shaped, but for hundreds of years they must have peopled the villages and the solitary farm-houses in the folds with stories of ghostly riders and unhappy ladies forever seeking their lost treasure. These ghosts have rambled about for so many centuries that they are now old inhabitants with family histories attached to them; but at the present moment one may find many phantoms hovering on the borderland of belief and scepti-cism – not yet believed in, but not properly accounted for. Human vanity, it may be, embodies them in the first place. The desire to be somehow impossibly, and therefore all the more mysteriously, concerned in secret affairs of national importance is very strong at the present moment. It is none of our business to supply reasons; only to notice queer signs, draw conclusions, and shake our heads. Each village has its wiseacre, who knows already more than he will say; and in a year or two who shall limit the circumstantial nar-ratives which will be current in the neighbourhood, and possibly masquerade in solemn histories for the instruction of the future!

In this district, for instance, there are curious ridges or shelves in the hillside, which the local antiquaries variously declare to have been caused by ice-pressure, or by the pick-axes of prehistoric man. But since the war we have made far better use of them. Not so very long ago, we say a hundred years at most, England was invaded, and, the enemy landing on the Down at the back of our village, we dug trenches to withstand him, much like those in use in Flanders now. You may see them with your own eyes. And this, somehow, is proof that if the Germans land they will land here, which, although terrifying, also gratifies our sense of our own importance.

But these historical speculations are for the contemplative mind of the shepherd, or of the old cottager, who can almost carry back to the days of the great invasion. His daughter has evidence of the supernatural state of things now existing without going farther than the shed in which her hens are sitting. When she came to hatch out her eggs, she will tell you, only five of the dozen had live chicks in them, and the rest were addled. This she attributes unhesitatingly to vibrations in the earth caused by the shock of the great guns in Flanders. If you express a doubt she will overwhelm you with evidence from all the country round. But no one here limits the action of the guns to the addling of a few hen's eggs; the very sun in the sky, they assert, has been somehow deranged in his mechanism by our thunder on earth. The dark spell of cloudy weather which spoilt July was directly due to these turmoils, and the weather-wise at the cottage laid it down as a fact that we should see no more sun all summer. None could rightly divine the reason; but to offer a reason for such sublime transactions would be almost to cast a doubt upon them. The sun has shone fiercely since then and is shining still, and local wisdom has fastened with renewed hope upon the behaviour of the church bell. The bell belongs to a church which stands solitary upon a hill in the midst of wild marshes, and is gifted with the power of foretelling the return of peace by dropping from the belfry exactly three months before peace is declared. Thus, at least, did it testify to the advent of peace after the Boer War; and once again, on 3 May last, to the delight of all beholders, the rope broke and the bell fell to earth.

August is well on its way, but you may still hear the guns from the top of the Downs; the sun blazes in a cloudless sky, and the eggs are no longer addled; but we are by no means downcast, and merely turn our minds to the next riddle, with deeper conviction than before that we live in a world full of mysteries.

Article in **The Times**, *15 August 1916*

In the Second World War the Woolfs' house at Rodmell, Monk's House, lay beneath the fighting-space of the Battle of Britain, and the flight path of German bombers to London.

Ought I not to look at the sunset rather than write this? A flush of red in the blue; the haystack in the marsh catches the glow; behind me, the apples are red in the trees. L. is gathering them. Now a plume of smoke goes from the train under [Mount] Caburn. And all the air a solemn stillness holds. till 8.30 when the cadaverous twanging in the sky begins; the planes going to London. Well its an hour to that. Cows feeding. The elm tree sprinkling its little leaves against the sky. Our pear tree swagged with pears; & the weathercock above the triangular church tower above it . . . Last night a great heavy plunge of bombs under the window. So near we both started. A plane had passed dropping this fruit. We went on to the terrace. Trinkets of stars sprinkled & glittering. All quiet . . . Caburn was crowned with what looked like a settled moth, wings extended – a Messerschmitt it was, shot down on Sunday.

Diary, 2 October 1940

There was an anti-aircraft battery on the hill behind Rodmell, and if one can judge by the pillboxes still standing there (one of them used as a store-hut for the sports ground) the village was intended to serve as a pocket of resistance in the event of a German invasion. Monk's House stood at the edge of the Ouse marshes, and these defence works were very close.

Early in November a German bomb burst the banks of the Ouse, and the marshland was flooded almost as far as Monk's House.

The haystack in the floods is of such incredible beauty . . . When I look up I see all the marsh water. In the sun deep blue, gulls caraway seeds: snowberries: atlantic flier: yellow islands: leafless trees: red cottage roofs. Oh may the flood last for ever . . .

Diary, 5 November 1940

This was Virginia's last happy passage of descriptive writing. Five months later, when the Ouse had retreated within its banks again, she drowned herself in its waters.

The Fenlands

Virginia Woolf had long associations with the Fenlands of eastern England. She had family and personal links with Cambridge and its university (that 'sanctuary in which are preserved rare types which would soon be obsolete if left to fight for existence on the pavement of the Strand'), and twice in her youth she spent long holidays in the Fen counties, whose great skies and clear light profoundly impressed her – 'such expanse & majesty & illuminations I have never seen. Pure air for fathoms & fathoms & acres & acres . . . .'.

A Visit to Warboys, Cambridgeshire, *1899*

. . . We came to Warboys Station, found our primitive Omnibus, & drove off the mile to the Rectory. It had been raining all the afternoon (the first rain I have seen for weeks) & the sky was all clouded & misted as for steady showers. However as we drove along the sun shot a shaft of light down; & we beheld a glorious expanse of sky – this golden gauze streamer lit everything in its light; & far away over the flat fields a spire caught the beam & glittered like a gem in the darkness & wetness of the surrounding countries. Let me remark that the village of Warboys runs

74

along the street for a mile to the gates of the Rectory; there are few shops, but we passed 4 windmills (attractive shaped things) & *Nine Public Houses.*

Diary, 4 August

Warboys is some six miles north-east of Huntingdon. The railway no longer goes there, and its nine pubs have been reduced to two. The rectory, which the Stephens had taken for their summer holiday, is now called the Moat House, and is much smaller than it was in Virginia's time – its present owners, Mr and Mrs Derek Gladwin, in restoring it to excellent condition after a long period of neglect, have pulled down most of the servants' quarters at the back. Virginia and her siblings spent much of their time messing around in a punt on the pond, which is still there.

This is a melancholy country. I went this afternoon with A. [Adrian, her younger brother] into the church opposite our gates. It is the church of St Mary Magdalene, & it was built in the 14th century. The churchyard is full of sombre tombstones, with queer carvings & angels heads sprawling over date & name & all. There are many graves that are nameless; & I was startled to think that I was walking over some ancient dust forgotten & undistinguished from the hillocks of the field. The graves rise in swelling mounds side by side all along the bottom of the churchyard.

Diary, 7 August

The graveyard still heaves with anonymous burial bumps, and its grass is kept down by two tethered goats. During the Second World War an airfield near Warboys was the base of the RAF's Pathfinder Force, and in the church there is now a stained-glass window in its memory.

All the land that was Fen is now cut up into innumerable cornfields. We beheld the harvesters this afternoon as we rode back from Ramsey. On one side of the road was a corn cutting machine sweeping down the standing corn; & on the other a field where corn lay all cut; & here & there women & boys were all tramping thro' it heaping the corn into stooks. Even a little child not more than 4 years old was harvesting with its mother. It wore a bright scarlet frock, & trotted behind with a small armful of gleanings. One of the women harvesters was I should think almost 70 with white scanty locks, & a wrinkled sun burnt wind scourged face. There is some picturesque element in this country − harvesters, windmills, golden cornfields. Everything flat with blue haze in the distance, & a vast dome of sky all around.

Diary, 8 August

I was one day walking in some fields near Warboys when someone called across a hedge to me − 'Can you tell me the right way to Warboys?' It happened that the road ran at some little distance, & though of course I could point the direction, I found it somewhat difficult to describe accurately the exact path by which it could be reached.

So as I could well shorten my walk & do the wondering voice a good turn, I called back 'if you will come over here, I will show you, as I myself am going back that way.' The voice seemed to hesitate, & then I heard a creaking of thorns & twigs, as though some body were being thrust relentlessly through a very fine specimen of the hawthorn hedge.

Diary, August (undated)

The people here are a peculiar race. So imbedded are they in their own delving pursuits, living lonely self contained lives, with a few strong religious opinions that only serve to narrow their minds, that a stranger is in their eyes a most contemptible creature. They are solid conservatives, & resent a stranger or an innovation in their lives. The Schoolmaster, who has been here 25 years, says he still feels out in the cold; they do not look upon him as one of themselves. The curate is a man of humour but humour has a hard battle of it in such surroundings. Nevertheless he told his Curates Recollections with great glee – jumping & jerking in a peculiar way he has when something amuses him.

Diary, 10 August

This is the midst of the old Fen country. This solid ground on which we stood was, not many years ago, all swamp & reed; now indeed there is a pathway, & on either side grow potatoes & corn, but the Fen character remains indelible A broad ditch crosses the Fen, in which there is cold brown water even in this hot summer. Tall rushes & water plants grow from it; & small white moths, the inhabitants of the Fens, were fluttering among them in scores when we were there. I wish that once & for all I could put down in this wretched handwriting how this country impresses me – how great I feel the stony-hard flatness & monotony of the plain. Every time I write in this book I find myself drifting into the attractive but impossible task of describing the Fens – till I grow heartily sick of so much feeble word painting; & long for one expressive quotation that should signify in its solitary compass all the glories of earth air & Heaven. Nevertheless I own it is a joy to me to be set down with such a vast never ending picture to reproduce – reproduction is out of the question – but to gaze at, nibble at & scratch at.

Diary, 12 August

Our journey from Warboys to Huntingdon is one of those not infrequent train journeys in this part of the world which are a splendid triumph for the bicycle. You can bicycle with comfort & pleasure into Huntingdon under an hour. It takes just the same to do the 8 miles in the train; & the fares moreover for the return journey of 3 people amount to 7s.6d. There are 2 changes at Somersham & at St Ives; & at the first of these stations we had to wait 10 minutes & at the 2nd 5. The first – Somersham train we waited for & caught comfortably. At St Ives we had to cross various platforms to reach the one which, the guard assured us, was the Huntingdon platform. We had only 5 minutes at this, so that we lost no time in running across & getting into position for our 3rd class carriage. We waited; no train or sign of a train; so we investigated the machinery of a sweet machine, which, proving defective in every branch, we retreated to the weighing machine. So 20 minutes passed; then we became uneasy & captured a paper boy – 'When does the Huntingdon train come in?' 'Oh at 2.15' said he – No, no, said Vanessa; I know there is a train at 12.43. The paper boy smiled somewhat grimly – The 12.43 has already been gone 20 minutes, Miss, said he – from the other platform.' We then had been intent upon the eccentricities of the sweet machine & the weighing machine while the train came in on the other side of us, took up its passengers & went on its way. It was now about 20 minutes past one. We ought to have arrived at 5 minutes past one – & we should arrive – when? I must say that when our faculties are effectually though rudely aroused by some emergency like this we take a practical view of the case. We spoke little, but decided in a few moments that a horse & cart must be found in St Ives capable of taking us with no delay to our Uncle & cousins at Godmanchester. We went to the County Arms; but this had long ago given up keeping traps we were told; then to the Robin Hood whose trap was just gone out; then to the Ramping Lion Inn, who did not possess a trap, & then to the Fountain – who did possess a trap – which trap could be at our service in 10 minutes. So we sat down in a little par-lour which smelt of wine – the Inn keeper came & sat with us to beguile the time. He was a young man, overflowing with good nature & talk. Before long he told us, what I guessed as soon as I saw him, that he was a stranger in these parts, & finds them terribly dull. On Mondays he said, we have a market, & then there's something doing, but on other days nothing happens ever. There never was such a sleepy place. He asked if we came from London – & when we said we did, he asked us many questions about London weather. Evidently a little change such as this was all the excitement he ever got. (This young man & the chemist are both people who testify to the character of the Fens & the Fen people. They are looked upon as strangers; & they on their side find the country, the people & the life terribly monotonous.) However soon our pony came to the door, & we started hastily. It is 5 miles to Godmanchester & it was now 25 minutes to 2. St Ives as we saw it driving through must just have one exclamation of admiration. It is all built along one winding cobble paved street. The river lies on the left; & St Ives crosses the river over the lengthy & beautiful bridge which has carried the name of St Ives into countries & towns far distant from Huntingdon. The last picture that I saw of it was in the Phillimores drawing room at the wedding party just a week before we came here. The bridge is an old stone bridge; its claim to distinction being that in the middle there is a square tower – for what purpose I do not know. (I will look up the History of St Ives & its bridge in Kelly, & write it on the opposite page.)

We drove our five miles through quaint old villages – such as I have never seen equalled. Everything is old – such antiquity grows depressing after a time; there is only one new house in Godmanchester, so we were told – a new house being a house that does not date back to the 17th century, & this house had to be new because the original old one was burnt down. We reached Godmanchester at 2.15 & found the party on the verge of lunch. To cut matters short we had lunch & then, in a sharp shower of rain, started for the boat . . .

Picture us uncomfortably seated on a towing path; half the party in a ditch, the other half in long grass – a cold wind blowing, with occasional drops of rain – no glow in east or west – but a grey melancholy vista of sky. Sir Herbert fought wasps & eat bread & jam – then we slowly packed our basket & started back for Godmanchester. I sat in one boat with Lady Stephen, & Adrian & Harry to row. We kept well ahead of the others. The rain fell now with a vengeance. We got back however in time to escape an absolute wet throughness.

So ended a somewhat grim day of pleasure.

Diary, 18 August (headed 'Warboys Distractions')

St Ives, in Cambridgeshire, might no longer raise exclamations of admiration in Virginia. A dingy and remarkably litter-strewn town in 1992, its cobbles have been removed and a large new road bridge crosses the River Ouse downstream from the old one – whose 'tower' was really a medieval chantry chapel upon which an extra storey (since removed) had been added to make a house of it. There are still very few new buildings in the centre of Godmanchester (when I drove into the town, as it happened, the only other vehicle moving down its main street was a steamroller) and its river front is still a popular starting place for boating excursions.

We met a Fen funeral coming back from Warboys, where the dead had been buried. There were about 5 bakers carts & a cart which had been used in carrying the corn, all filled with men & women dressed in deep mourning. They came from the east along the absolutely straight white road. We saw them crawling towards us with the sky heaping clouds & the wind blowing blue spaces around them. As we passed them, a boy looked down at us very sullenly & with the peculiar sodden depressed look that Fen men & women have; they were absolutely silent; & the procession went on to the heart of the Fen. I dreamt most vividly of this last night; how I looked into the womens faces; & the carts passed on & on into the [night?] they were going back to some strange dark land, & they said the only time they saw the light of day was when they came to Warboys to bury their dead.

Diary, 4 September

Well then farewell Warboys. The summer ranks among our happiest I think; & this land of plain & sky will remain a distinct & lovely picture in my mind were I never to see it again.

Goodbye to Fens & flat fields & windmills & sky domes.

Diary, 21 September

Norfolk Holiday
Journal, August 1906

For the month of August 1906, Virginia and her sister Vanessa rented Blo' Norton Hall, near the hamlet of East Harling in Norfolk.

Nothing of our own day could reproduce the harmony & exquisite peace of this little old house, as it struck our eyes, yesterday evening. It is so modest, & sound, & solid all through; as tho' the centuries had only confirmed its original virtues. As you were made honestly, they seem to say, so all time to come shall but prove & establish your virtue.

And such domestic beauty, all small & quaint & even humble as it is, appeals to ones sympathies. It is so good to find that humdrum people should live so respectably; beauty & splendour were then not for the surface alone, but they sank down & down, till all layers of the state were well steeped in them. A self respecting decorous place England must have been then! ... few English people, I think, could endure such a dose [of antiquity] as Blo' Norton Hall is prepared to give them, without being drowned in it. We are to begin with 7 miles from a railway; & every mile seems to draw a thicker curtain than the last between you & the world. So that finally, when you are set down at the Hall, no sound what ever reaches your ear; the very light seems to filter through deep layers; & the air circulates slowly, as though it had but to make the circuit of the Hall, & its duties were complete.

Nor have such investigations as we could make today pierced behind the curtain. We seem to be in the middle of what in geography is called an 'undulating plain' well cultivated, but, apparently, almost deserted. The corn brims the fields; but no one is there to cut it; the churches hold up broad gray fingers all over the landscape, but no one, save perhaps the dead at their feet, attend to their commands; the windmills sail round & round, but no one trims their sails; it is very characteristic that the only sign of life in the land should be that produced by the wind of Heaven. How sleepy & ancient a people must be, who rely on the free gifts of Heaven still. But the wind seems fairly competent; the sails turn slowly, all day long. This, need I say it, is the kind of rash note an impetuous traveller makes; & it is only made because after all, such notes are the things one thinks before one begins to reason or to know. And like the images of childhood, they stay bright.

Blo' Norton is a moated timber-framed Tudor or Elizabethan house which had been, until his death in 1894, the property of the Maharajah Duleep Singh, a great favourite of Queen Victoria's. Duleep Singh had acquired Elveden Hall, a far grander house nearby, and had made of its 17,000 acres one of the great sporting properties in England: presumably he used Blo' Norton as a guest-house. Today, divided into two homes, the house remains wonderfully secluded down an avenue of beeches, its garden and moat in a gentlemanly degree of desuetude. When I called in 1992 the occupants I met had not known of Virginia's stay there.

The fens almost surround this house. And all the land is very flat, so that the landmarks resolve themselves into churches & windmills. The river, the Little Ouse deserves its diminutive; you may leap it – fall in as I did this afternoon – but all the same it is not a hazardous jump. You are sure of the mud at any rate. And there radiate various minor tributaries, ditches I should call them, did not I know of their relationship with the river, & these are sometimes fenced with barbed wire. Altogether, though a walk in the fen has a singular charm, it is not to be undertaken as a way of getting to places. Windmills have a way of staying absolutely still, or receding, to one who approaches them thus.

However, after leaping & circumnavigating, & brushing through reeds, & scrambling beneath barbed wire, it is pleasant to lie on the turf & try steering by windmills & towers to indicate on the map where you are precisely. Today I found the twin sources of the Waveney & the Little Ouse.

The windmills have gone, the church towers remain, the fens have largely been drained as cornlands, and a road just south of the village of Gasthorpe crosses, by a bridge, the reedy, weedy, brown and waterfowly source of the two rivers.

In a very short time unfortunately, it becomes clear how shortsighted was that opinion of mine that Norfolk had no inhabitants. It is not necessary here to go into details, which would be impolite; so I will only make the innocent remark that directly you begin to study the habits of creatures they become astonishingly frequent & well ordered. Here, it seems, one needs only but very little trouble in order to discover a whole net work of society – Squires & Parsons & detached ladies living in cottages, who are all entertaining & paying calls, far more punctually & assiduously than in London.

But it is more to the point to remark that I found the real heath, not a mile from our door. It is a wild place, all sand & bracken, with innumerable rabbits, & great woods running alongside, in to which I plunge; down green drives as shady as any in the New Forest. It is a strange lonely kind of country; a carriage comes bowling over the hill, & you watch it pass & disappear & wonder where it comes from & whither it goes, & who is the lady inside.

Shall I confess, without meaning any kind of confession, that it is possible for one day to be much like another here, & not in the least dull?

I go for my usual walk; which has for me the interest of a discovery, because I go, armed with maps into a strange land. Windmills are my landmarks; & one must not mistake the river for a ditch. The heath attracts me most; because there are no fields. The fen plays you false at every step – I walked through a jungle of reeds & fell up to my nose in mud. And if one foundered here, the weeds would wave & the plover call, & no robin redbreast would bury one!

If this were the time or the place to uphold a paradox, I am half inclined to state that Norfolk is one of the most beautiful of counties. Indeed, let the artifice stand; for so there will be no need to expound it. And truly, it would need a careful & skilful brush to give a picture of this strange, grey green, undulating, dreaming, philosophising & remembering land; where one may walk 10 miles & meet no one; where soft grass paths strike gently over the land; where the roads are many & lonely, & the churches are innumerable, & deserted. There is no use in a closer gaze at present. But it is worth saying that the more you walk here, & become initiated into the domesticities of the place – it is full of them – the more you love it, & know it. And that says as much for a place as for a person.

Yesterday, I took a bicycle ride to a place called Kenninghall . . . Now Kenninghall is famous in the Ordnance map for a Saxon burial ground . . . but . . . the Christian church alone was obvious; the curiously moulded tower, with its gilt clock, showed itself most decorously gray against the soft plumage of the trees . . .

So on the authority of the map, we asked a small native for his Saxon burial ground, & were directed by him to the Christian Churchyard; Saxons they may have been to him; &, to the shame of Kenninghall be it spoken, no one there not even the photographer, knew where the Saxons were buried; or indeed had ever heard that there were Saxons. So taking the map's word for it, we decided to consecrate a mound in some gentleman's Park; certainly I could see no reason why Saxons should not have been buried there.

But as one had to climb a gate, & walk half a mile, we decided to do our conjectural meditations from a distance . . .

Some eighty-six years later I had similar difficulties in finding the Saxons of Kenninghall: I settled for the same mound in the same gentleman's Park (now mostly ploughed or under conifers), and I did not climb the gate, either.

A very hot August day, a bare road across a moor, fields of corn & stubble – a haze as of wood fire smoke – innumerable pheasants & partridges – white stones – thatched cottages – sign posts – tiny villages – great waggons heaped with corn – sagacious dogs, farmers carts. Compose these all somehow into a picture; I am too lazy to do it.

At any rate after an hour's riding I dropped down into Thetford, which seemed to me with its girdle of wall & river, & the smooth turf slope outside something like an Italian town. Perhaps the knowledge extracted from the guide book that there was a nunnery here in the Middle Ages helped my imagination. Certainly I saw with my own eyes a Roman Catholic Padre step out of his monastery door, with a biretta on his head, & examine with long ecclesiastical nose the Dahlias in his neighbours garden. The rivers Thet & Ouse (I think) circle Thetford; & which ever way I went, seemed to take me across low stone bridges where anglers lounged, with their rods across the broad stream. Nursemaids were sitting on the rivers banks, leaning on the elbow over a paper novel, while their charges dabbled in the water. No one was ever able to say exactly what does go on in these medieval towns set in the heart of

England at about this hour on a Summers afternoon. It is all so picturesque & accidental that to the traveller it seems a pleasant show got up for some benevolent purpose. For when you come upon stalwart men leaning their elbows on a parapet & dreaming of the stream beneath, while the sun is still high in the air, you reconsider what you mean by life. Often in London shall I think of Thetford, & wonder if it is still alive; or whether it has really ceased, peaceably, to exist any longer. No one would notice if the whole town forgot to wake up one morning.

Thetford does not look very Italian now but to the stranger is still inexplicably set amongst its waters. Virginia had perhaps been reading Dickens on Venice: 'I have, many and many a time, thought since, of this strange Dream upon the water: half-wondering if it lie there yet . . . '

The New Forest

Virginia Woolf had known the New Forest since childhood, and in her twenties spent two Christmases there. She was not, however, very fond of the place.

The forest is too benign & complaisant; it gives you all that you can ask; but it hints at no more. There are the long green drives, & the tracery of the branches against the sky; there are wild open spaces when you are tired of symmetry, with their single elm & thorn trees, & their brambles & their bogs. 'So wild – so free – so stately – so mediaeval:' Such is the praise that you must give, & give willingly, but there is no residue that remains unexpressed for lack of the fitting word. To be candid the forest is a little sleek & a little tame; it is Saxon without any Celtic mysticism; it is flaxen & florid, stately & ornamental. We have no use for forests now, & yet this one is preserved reverently, when the old spirit has died out of it. So it comes about that there is always something artificial about the place, & its lovers. You will not find the real country man or woman here, anymore than you will find arduous fields that are still turned assiduously. No; the country labourers are wont to pose as characters learned in forest lore; & it is a lore that is consciously picturesque. Much of this attitude is probably inevitable, for the forest is different from any other piece of England, & imposes different customs of necessity. It is easy, for example, or so I have found it, to feel yourself withdrawn from the outer world, & enclosed in a thick girdle of trees. The rolling land is fenced off, & you are forced through narrow ways between trees where ever you turn. Then there is all the peculiar language of the place to be learnt if you stay, & exalted beyond all others. You hunt, the deer & the fox: there is the old colonel of course who never misses a meet & knows his way through the forest better than any of the tufters; such old gentlemen are not unusual, but in other countries surely they have fewer grooves in which to run so smoothly. The forest is an ideal place for the old & conservative; there are so many pro-prieties to be observed, & they are so decorous & easy of approach. So this is why Christmas is kept so appropriately here. You can almost fancy that the woods have been arranged for the festival, & hung with holly, & sprinkled with snow. Christmas day & the forest seemed to mix & melt indistinguishably; you left the dinner table & its turkey & its crackers, its cake with a jaunty sprig of holly in it – you stepped into a world where these emotions were continued unbrokenly. We walked along a crisp white road, & then beneath dark leaved ever greens. Here were berries glowing red; & all the twigs were iced with snow. Then it grew late & the jolly evening sky lit up – flame coloured, & clear & healthy – with the black trees sharp against it. But O for the dusky roll of some Northern moor, or the melancholy cliffs of Cornwall. There you hear the wind & the sea.

Diary, Christmas 1906

Virginia and her sister Vanessa had been staying at the home of their aunt Sarah Duckworth, described by Quentin Bell in his biography of Virginia Woolf as 'a rich, fat old lady and entirely commonplace', at Bank, on the outskirts of Lyndhurst: the house, Lane End, now displays a plaque recording Virginia's residence there.

An outing to Christchurch, during an earlier stay at Lane End, inspired one of Virginia Woolf's rare published travel essays.

You see Christchurch from afar like a ship riding out to sea. The land all round is flat as water; if the sun shines it may light up a little gleam of river or of the sea itself, because, as soon appears, the church is almost an island in the midst of waters. The sun when we made our expedition was not visible, but in spite of that the whole air was full of light. It was as though a white curtain had been drawn across the sky, by which the sunbeams as they fell were filtered to a pure white light. There was on the horizon a rim of sky like tarnished silver, but, otherwise, there was no slit in the curtain. The town of Christchurch resolves itself into one long street, which rises very slightly, and bursts at the top into its flower, which is the Priory Church. The church is built on the pattern of a small cathedral, and, perhaps, because of its comparative insignificance, has suffered very little from reformers and restorers. The stonework within has worn very white, and has crumbled in places, but for the most part the chiselling is as sharp as though it had just left the mason's hand. Much of the carving is of exquisite delicacy, and so perfect that one needs the assurance of the date inscribed on it to realise that the work is more than three hundred years old. But the most beautiful possession of the old church – and it has many both beautiful and curious – is the view from the square tower. Here out on the leads, with the sharp spine of the church running out beneath you, you look to the sea on two sides; and directly at your feet the rivers Stour and Avon loop and cross and entangle themselves like a silver chain. The church is one of the few great churches that has not chosen to plant itself on a hill; the stream laps at its feet, and it looks as though an extra large wave would roll across the land and break against the church walls. Only a breadth of flats, dun-coloured with feathery bulrushes, separates the land from the water; looking east there is no hill, and on the horizon an undulating shadow marks the beginning of the New Forest.

Essay in the Guardian, *26 July 1905*

The Yorkshire Moors

Virginia Woolf twice visited Giggleswick, in the north Yorkshire moors, where her cousin Will Vaughan was headmaster of Giggleswick School. During her first visit, when she stayed at the headmaster's house, she made an expedition across the moors to Haworth, the home of the Brontës, and her description of it was her first published article.

'Haworth'
Essay in the Guardian, *21 December 1904*

. . . Our excitement as we neared Haworth had in it an element of suspense that was really painful, as though we were to meet some long-separated friend, who might have changed in the interval – so clear an image of Haworth had we from print and picture. At a certain point we entered the valley, up both sides of which the village climbs, and right on the hill-top, looking down over its parish, we saw the famous oblong tower of the church. This marked the shrine at which we were to do homage.

It may have been the effect of a sympathetic imagination, but I think that there were good reasons why Haworth did certainly strike one not exactly as gloomy, but, what is worse for artistic purposes, as dingy and commonplace. The houses, built of yellow-brown stone, date from the early nineteenth century. They climb the moor step by step in little detached strips, some distance apart, so that the town instead of making one compact blot on the landscape has contrived to get a whole stretch into its clutches. There is a long line of houses up the moor-side, which clusters round the church and parsonage with a little clump of trees. At the top the interest for a Brontë lover becomes suddenly intense. The church, the parsonage, the Brontë Museum, the school where Charlotte taught, and the Bull Inn where Branwell drank are all within a stone's throw of each other. The museum is certainly rather a pallid and inanimate collection of objects. An effort ought to be made to keep things out of these mausoleums, but the choice often lies between them and destruction, so that we must be grateful for the care which has preserved much that is, under any circumstances, of deep interest. Here are many autograph letters, pencil drawings, and other documents. But the most touching case – so touching that one hardly feels reverent in one's gaze – is that which contains the little personal relics, the dresses and shoes of the dead woman. The natural fate of such things is to die before the body that wore them, and because these, trifling and transient though they are, have survived, Charlotte Brontë the woman comes to life, and one forgets the chiefly memorable fact that she was a great writer. Her shoes and her thin muslin dress have outlived her. One other object gives a thrill; the little oak stool which Emily carried with her on her solitary moorland tramps, and on which she sat, if not to write, as they say, to think what was probably better than her writing.

The church, of course, save part of the tower, is renewed since Brontë days; but that remarkable churchyard remains. The old edition of the *Life* had on its title-page a little print which struck the keynote of the book; it seemed to be all graves – gravestones stood ranked all round; you walked on a pavement lettered with dead names; the graves had solemnly invaded the garden of the parsonage itself, which was as a little oasis of life in the midst of the dead. This is no exaggeration of the artist's, as we found: the stones seem to start out of the ground at you in tall, upright lines, like an army of silent soldiers. There is no hand's breadth untenanted; indeed, the economy of space is somewhat irreverent. In old days a flagged path, which suggested the slabs of graves, led from the front door of the parsonage to the churchyard without interruption of wall or hedge; the garden was practically the graveyard too; the successors of the Brontës, however, wishing a little space between life and death, planted a hedge and several tall trees, which now cut off the parsonage garden completely. The house itself is precisely the same as it was in Charlotte's day, save that one new wing has been added. It is easy to shut the eye to this, and then you have the square, boxlike parsonage, built of the ugly, yellow-brown stone which they quarry from the moors behind, precisely as it was when Charlotte lived and died there. Inside, of course, the changes are many, though not such as to obscure the original shape of the rooms. There is nothing remarkable in a mid-Victorian parsonage, though tenanted by genius, and the only room which awakens curiosity is the kitchen, now used as an ante-room, in which the girls tramped as they conceived their work. One other spot has a certain grim interest – the oblong recess beside the staircase into which Emily drove her bulldog during the famous fight, and pinned him while she pommelled him. It is otherwise a little sparse parsonage, much like others of its kind. It was due to the courtesy of the present incumbent that we were allowed to inspect it; in his place I should often feel inclined to exorcise the three famous ghosts.

One thing only remained: the church in which Charlotte worshipped, was married, and lies buried. The circumference of her life was very narrow. Here, though much is altered, a few things remain to tell of her. The slab which bears the names of the succession of children and of their parents – their births and deaths – strikes the eye first.

Name follows name; at very short intervals they died – Maria the mother, Maria the daughter, Elizabeth, Branwell, Emily, Anne, Charlotte, and lastly the old father, who outlived them all. Emily was only thirty years old, and Charlotte but nine years older. 'The sting of death is sin, and the strength of sin is the law, but thanks be to God which giveth us the victory through our Lord Jesus Christ.' That is the inscription which has been placed beneath their names, and with reason; for however harsh the struggle, Emily, and Charlotte above all, fought to victory.

Haworth is now one of Yorkshire's chief tourist attractions, largely perhaps because of the film Wuthering Heights, *which beat* Gone with the Wind *for its Oscar as best film of the year in 1939. In summer the town is almost overwhelmed by the pressure of cars and coaches – only the main street has been reserved for pedestrians – and it is rich in phenomena like the Brontë Taxi Service and the Wuthering Heights Free House. The Brontë Museum, housed in Virginia's day on the first floor above the Yorkshire Penny Bank (now the Tourist Information Office), has been transferred to the parsonage itself. The town still retains, however, a certain moorland atavism. When I was there in 1992 a gang of small boys, one of them an Arab, one black, were throwing sticks for conkers into the horse-chestnut tree in the yard of the Baptist chapel, while inside the church a leafless branch of a tree was stuck with scribbled prayers: 'Please Let Me Be Mark Aspin's Girl Friend', or 'Please Let Me And My Sister Be Friends Again'.*

The statesman R.B.Haldane, asked his opinion of Virginia's essay about Haworth, observed: 'What merits – but I think the writer can get still more inside her subject.'

Walking the Moors
Journal, April 1906

During Virginia's second visit to Giggleswick she stayed in lodgings in the town, and spent her days walking.

In a placid & matter of fact frame of mind the solitary traveller starts on his journey. If you are one you have so strangely little to think about; your wants are so easily satisfied. So, then, smoothly & unlaboriously I travelled from one end of England to the other today, asked but little information, found trains & carriages, directed my luggage, & deposited everything at Mrs. Turners, in Giggleswick, delightfully late – because it mattered to no one.

It is just that scrupulously clean, prosaic lodging I wished; & so far my solitude has been exquisite, & delightfully amusing. When will I dine? When will I breakfast? I settle precisely according to my own taste, & then the door is shut on me, & I may read for two hours peacefully if I like. The only sound that distracts me is the Northern Express shooting to Edinburgh.

For this is no smug suburban lodging, beneath a park door; the moors rise in waves all round; great crags of rock make a back ground, dimly seen in the April twilight & wild scents of the moor are driven in at the open window.

It is a discreet little Northern town, swept clean & simplified, out of all pettiness & vulgarity by the nobility of the country in which it lies.

Giggleswick has changed very little – the expresses for Scotland still pass nearby, though they are probably less noisy than the steam trains that disturbed Virginia – but when I enquired in 1992 I was unable to unearth any memories of Mrs Turner and her lodgings.

The moors are given up entirely to sheep, & are intersected by stone walls, no tree or hedge grows on them. Here and there you see a bleak stone house on the hill side, in which the shepherd lives. In many ways this land is like Cornwall; but I have not time to determine the differences.

All the sheep had their lambs, & were therefore bold & even defiant.

You find strange fortifications on the moors, fosses & ramparts, so smoothly built & carpeted that either nature was the architect, or some primeval man.

The contrast is part of the charm. You walk upon very gentle downs, which fold themselves into steep hollows, & are fringed with slender groves of trees. It is an undulating, & suave country, lacking the abrupt majesty of the moors, but excelling them in a certain charm; a kind of pathos from its more immediate connection with low human kind. One gray farm, with its walled garden, will do much to humanise a whole sweep of field & down. And by that one means here, perhaps, something by no means cheerful & domestic, but melancholy & appealing rather; for the land remains a half tame thing; with all & wild creatures fearing for freedom in its eyes.

For 2 hours I met no single person; but listened to the queer cries & laments of plovers & curlews, wheeling close above my head, for the afternoon was almost cloudless, & singularly warm.

All the trees here are red & purple, but not green yet. It is not a country that is very sensitive to changes of the season I imagine. In winter it looked much the same. Two thousand years ago it looked as it did this afternoon; in that continuity lies its singular grandeur & stability perhaps. Two thousand years again may leave it equally unchanged.

Today the singular & rather pleasant phenomenon was seen of great white flakes of snow falling across a deep blue

sky. But they were merely tentative, or decorative, &
ceased by midday. In the afternoon however, walking to
Lawkland, there was a bright light of white on the top of
Ingleborough; which indeed is majestic enough to veil his
crown in the clouds occasionally. It was a lovely walk,
along the valley. We met a shepherd digging mournfully at
a drain which cuts across the road. One of the lambs, apparently, had run into the funnel of this thing, which
stretched into the fields; & had gone probably too far to be
dug out alive: A tuft of wool on the briar showed where he
was lost. The minute & anxious care with which every
separate lamb in the flock is watched surprises the stranger;
the lambs seem so innumerable, & their destinies so un-
important. But every field, did one know it, is full of these
details which are important facts to an experienced eye.

Lawkland is an old Manor House; too small to be restored, & thus a beautiful specimen of simple domestic
building, standing just off the road where every one may
see it. All its graceful gables, & worn traceries are there untouched; & it is flanked by rough farm houses, of an earlier
date still perhaps. You see how neatly self sufficient the old
house was – & still, perhaps, remote in the Yorkshire moors
as it is, needs all its resources.

The Matrons of Giggleswick sat in conclave this afternoon upon the scheme for boarding out poor children.
Substantial squiresses, ruling their broad acres with capable
thumb, parsons' wives, village gossips, &c. &c.; but the
Yorkshire type of gentry is distinguished, & decided. They
had come driving in from distant Halls & Parsonage, & rattled off again, in dog carts & high gigs.

*Lawkland is still there for all to see, unmistakable beside the road,
and still with a curious air of remoteness.*

Today was memorable at least for a really successful walk,
to a place called Feizor – a wizard like name . . .

We got into a strange vale between two moors; all turf,

with flocks & herds feeding there, but no house or human creature. It stretched a long way, sequestered from wind or any blast from the outside world, a dreamlike hollow between gray moors; & finally we looked down upon Feizor, a little village of farm houses, a centre, I suppose for this pasturage land.

I thought what an odd fate it was to live in an old stone house all the days of one's life in the village of Feizor when the whole of the world lies open to one. The road which joins it to the main line is grown with grass; & as we walked along it, we came upon tinkers of some kind, making a shelter out of the hood of a cart; & ranging their household goods in the ditch – They sprang up & asked us for matches, had I been alone it would have been unpleasant. You could see the elemental look of demand in the mans face; as though it were his natural instinct to ask other people to supply him. The great melancholy moors, sweeping all round us, like some tragic audience, or chorus, mutely attendant, grew black, & veiled with mist. Rain came down, & the country seemed well pleased at this change of mood. Storm & rough weather suit it better than bland & innocent skies. But words! words! You will find nothing to match the picture.

Feizor remains one of the most secluded and enchanting villages of the Yorkshire moorlands. It is now a well-known base for walkers, but except for a new house or two must be very much as it was in Virginia Woolf's day – there is a ford across the river in the village street, and even the side-road that leads there is still grassy.

Wiltshire

Journal, August 1903

*For their summer holiday of 1903 the Stephen family rented Neth-
erhampton House, in the village of Netherhampton near Wilton
in Wiltshire.*

The house is exactly what I expected – & hoped. The front
view – we look on to the road – is of a little gray stone
house, too humble to be itself ornate, but evidently dating
from an ornate period – & in its humble way an imitation of
a genuine great house. There is some kind of architectural
device of urns at intervals on the gables; there is a hollowed
recess in the wall, meant perhaps, were the thing on a
larger scale, to stand a statue in. The garden gate, too, is un-
common – gracefully wrought in blue green iron, &
surmounted by a coat of arms & a crest. This house, as a
matter of fact, was built in Elizabeths time I think, as dower
houses to the Pembroke family; the coat of arms, besides
various small statelinesses within & without, proclaim its
aristocratic connections; various old countesses & depen-
dent relatives have had their lodging here, after the
splendours of Wilton [House] – though at the present time
it is no longer used for this purpose. The Furses who have it

now have done their decorating &c. in entire sympathy
with the character of the place – The wide rooms are furnished not too profusely with the dignified chairs, & solid
tables: crimson & white is the scheme of the whole place,
with a touch of ruddy old wood. It is, I feel, a very characteristic English country house of the more modest sort;
solid & unpretentious, but with a certain quaint dignity of
its own, greatly mellowed by time. These little gray old
houses are common all over England, but I doubt whether
you find them elsewhere – I have not had time to see much
of the garden – but it looks in keeping with the house – a
walled kitchen garden – broad grass walks – a sundial – all
on a small useful scale – kitchen garden teeming with fruit
& vegetables – but of a comfortable airy kind.

*Netherhampton House is a delightful but decidedly peculiar
house, being an amalgam of sixteenth-century cottage, a modest
seventeenth-century house and a remarkable façade – 'amazing',
Nikolaus Pevsner called it – which was evidently added in the
eighteenth century, and which does indeed, as Virginia said,
make it seem like an imitation great house. It is still the property
of the Pembroke family of Wilton, but in 1992 was being kept in
admirable trim by its lessee, Mr John Parnaby.*

Yesterday, or the day before, we set off after breakfast to
find out our position in the world. Our garden is really only
a bit of the meadow shorn & cut off from the rest of the
fields by a sunk fence. The house is very long & low, but the
front view gives really no idea of its size; it turns round &
makes a square court moreover, & only the face of the
house is gray. The rest – & older part – is built of red brick.
We had some curiosity to find the river, & the village of
Wilton – our difficulty was to decide which of the many
streams we met was the river – in time though we came to
such a broad & vigorous stream that we decided to name it
the Wylye & count the smaller rivulets which cut up the
meadows as mere tributaries – trained to flow thus in order

to water the fields. Indeed a most elaborate system of canals, & hatches, & little waterfalls is arranged all over the meadows, but the water is now for the most part cut off, & the meadows are dry. We tramped along the road finally, which is on one side walled off by a very high & neatly preserved brick wall. Inside lie the gardens of Wilton – miles & miles of them, I should judge, by the time it took us to trudge this side of their boundaries. At last we turned the corner, & came, very obviously, to the Great Gate of Wilton. It is made in the shape of a Roman Arch – though whether it is surmounted by the figure of a Roman Emperor, or whether one of the Earls of Pembroke has been clad in a toga for the occasion, I can not say.

The other statue, just outside the gates suggests that the modern military uniform at any rate is not the right stuff for bronze: The sculptor, moreover, in respect for the nobility of his sitter has made him at least 3 feet taller than the most gigantic of ordinary mortals. As a work of art therefore, the statue is not convincing; but when one reads the inscription at the base one understands that a very heroic figure was needed. After this we walked through the town. There are moods when the little old South of England town, with its peace & quaintness are entirely refreshing: there are times when its eternal sameness – its somnolence as of one that has fallen asleep of a surfeit of roast beef & plum pudding – are depressing. I am craving, I think, for the bareness & warmth & brilliance of a foreign land. But Wilton is particularly apt to excite this kind of discontent; it is more smug & well pleased with itself than the majority of English villages like all those in small hamlets that sit in the shadow of a great house. It has the look of a very faithful old family retainer – as I have no doubt those that live in its cottages are – pensioned off by the great people & unswervingly loyal to them. Its whole world is circled by the 'Park'; its interest is concerned entirely with 'Her Ladyship' & the goings on at the Castle. In almost every street you can trace the influence of the Herbert family. The three inns are of course loyally christened after

the various titles of the Pembrokes; their arms, slightly battered by weather hang from all the sign posts: they, in their
turn, have scattered fountains & almshouses all round
them, & generally keep the village so tidy & sweet that it
makes the most respectable setting for Wilton itself.

We – that is Adrian & I – commented upon all this – in
no very friendly spirit. We professed to find the whole
country side 'demoralised' & clinging to the great man of
the place. This I suppose is an exaggeration; at any rate if
we had been inside those high brick walls our point of view
might have changed – but it is safe to say that the feudal
spirit in England is not yet dead.

*The Great Gate (which is in fact presided over by the Emperor
Marcus Aurelius) is the main entrance to Wilton House, since the
sixteenth century the seat of the Earls of Pembroke. The statue outside, of the 13th Earl, does indeed have a heroic inscription to live
up to: it attributes to His Lordship fearlessness, singleness of soul,
the will always to strive for wisdom, piety, love of lonely study,
humbleness, uprightness, truthfulness, slowness unto wrath,
equanimity, charity, tenderness, patience, fortitude, purity and a
mild, modest and grave bearing. The Pembroke family is still
powerful in Wilton, if only because it owns much of the village,
but I suspect the feudal spirit has long waned: only one of the six
pubs is now named after the Pembrokes, and when in 1992 I remarked to a passing citizen that the village's long association with
the family was very fascinating, she remarked coolly: 'I suppose it
is, if you're interested in that kind of thing . . . '*

Adrian, with his wonderful faculty for finding something
wrong in his immediate circumstances – whatever they are
– grumbled the whole time at the dulness of the country –
in which I conceive he is wholly wrong. Such genuine
country I conceive can never be dull; even though nature
here hasn't taken much pains apparently with her material.
She has kept a charm though which is entirely absent in
more obviously interesting places. As we drove along

through lanes deeply cut in the chalk, I kept likening the downs to the long curved waves of the sea. It is as though the land here, all molten once, & rolling in vast billows had solidified while the waves were still swollen & on the point of breaking. From a height it looks as though the whole land were flowing. Man, too, has done nothing to change the shape of these breakers. He has planted them to a certain extent, but has mostly left their grass untouched for his flocks. You see a thatched shed or so on the down side where the shepherd lives, but no other human house. The villages have all sunk into the hollows between the waves; & the result is a peculiar smoothness & bareness of outline. This is the bare bone of the earth . . .

We are still exploring. Yesterday I took Nessa across the water meadows to a certain romantic looking church – at least that was our intention . . . We were brought to a stop by hearing male rustic voices, alarming to pedestrians of the womanly sex – Men were making hay in the adjoining field & not only were they talking but they were talking of us – possibly to us. Seeing us stop, one of them advanced to the gate; we had to move up to hear what he said. He was evidently jocular – & we thought it best to anticipate any remarks he might have to make by asking boldly our way out? 'Your fairly lost, you are' he said – which seemed to tickle him a good deal. 'Where d'you want to go?' It seemed idiotic to say nowhere – so I prompted Nessa – 'the Road' 'The Road?' 'You dont mean to say you've lost the road in broad daylight?' That was an excellent joke too – 'You wont find no road here – better go back the way you come' And so we turned & went – It was shouted after us that the sleek brown cows feeding at the other end of the field were dangerous – but we took no heed.

Small red houses have marched out in the van & rear of Salisbury, as of every other town, combining, I imagine their architect to say, the advantages of a Cathedral city with pure country air. Any other combination would be preferable I think. I had made the spire my aim – now I grazed as close it as I could – invaded the sanctuaries of the Close indeed, where motor cars may not penetrate, or butchers carts, unless bearing clerical provisions. The close is the same as all Cathedral closes – very rich, very peaceful – with the air of a very comfortably cushioned Sanctuary from the sins & weariness of the outer world. The old ladies who let their dresses sweep its turf are infected by the atmosphere; they move with extreme leisure & dignity – as though earthly affairs had no longer any power to hurry them. Yet I can well imagine that their precincts cover as much scandal of an innocent sort as any similar space in Mayfair or Belgravia. It is a picturesque but relaxing little haven, I am sure, & the Bishop & Chapter would do much better turned out of their spacious Georgian houses, & made to share the common lot. I should suggest that the close, shut against Butcher carts & motor cars by all means, should remain open to people of a literary disposition – who lodged at their ease in Palace & Deanery, would certainly turn their luxury to account.

The neighbourhood of the Cathedral though is depressing. So much ancient stone however fairly piled, & however rich with the bodies of Saints & famous men, seems to suck the vitality of its humble neighbours. It is like a great forest oak; nothing can grow healthily beneath its shade.

Salisbury now has a population of 37,000, and on a weekend evening can still seem fairly devitalised, with its tumbled rubbish and its huddles of apparently disaffected youth. Some people of a literary disposition, including a former Prime Minister, are now lodged in the Close, but the Bishop and the Dean are still in situ.

There is no denying – if you pretend to be a person of culture – that Salisbury Cathedral is beautiful – & culture or not, I honestly feel it to be so. It grows upon one; you find your eye wandering over the landscape to look for it: & when you find it, you keep your eye there for some moments satisfied. We are on a level with Salisbury – & no hills lie between us. I have not yet in my walks passed beyond its range. Sometimes I see the point of its spire – like an extinguisher – sitting on the side of the down. Oftenest I see it across the meadows – the whole church planted firm there – solid, & yet exquisitely light & graceful at once. It takes all kinds of tones – sometimes it is a pale gray – then almost white; today, for some reason it looked as though built of dark brown stone. George [her half-brother, George Duckworth] & I meant to spend a part of our Sunday appropriately in worship within its walls – but decided that afternoon service, drawn out by sermon &c., was too great an expense of time. So we invented (as it turned out) an Evensong at 7 to suit our purpose, & drove over in time for that. But the first youth we stopped in the Close pointed out our mistake – for some reason, Salisbury Cathedral provides no Evensong. Our only way of worship therefore – & a thoroughly happy one – was to drive slowly round the close. In certain moods I know, this kind of thing is intolerable; I would no more live here than lie myself down tomorrow in a venerable grave in the cloisters; but no place can be more amply satisfactory to spend an hour in – It is as though you shut thick ivy grown walls between yourself & the world; within them all is ancient loveliness & peace. English Cathedrals have certainly one inestimable advantage over the only foreign ones that I have seen; they stand in a perfect garden of their own, whereas the great French churches open on to the street. Here, for instance the Cathedral is circled by a rich layer of turf – & beyond that, like a zealous bodyguard, stand round all the houses of the close. These harmonise so perfectly with the prevailing spirit of the Cathedral that you hardly notice them individually till you stop especially to do so. They seem to me to act, I say, as a kind of bodyguard: nothing vulgar shall taint the air of the cathedral; they treasure up &

absorb the precious incense it gives out. And like the beef-eaters, or some other ancient guard, they are eminently picturesque without rivalling the splendour of their monarch.

It was proposed in 1992 that Salisbury Cathedral should accept the commercial sponsorship of McDonalds, the hamburger chain.

We now came out on the top of Salisbury plain, & the downs spread without check for miles round us. I suddenly looked ahead, & saw with the start with which one sees in real life what ones eye has always known in pictures, the famous circle of Stonehenge. Pictures give one no idea of size; & I had imagined something on a much larger scale. I had thought that the stones were scattered at intervals over a great space of the plain – so that when we settled to meet the riders at 'Stonehenge' I had privately judged the plan to be far too vague. But really it is a tiny compact little place . . . otherwise the pictures had prepared me fairly truthfully – as to shape & position that is; I had not realised though that the stones have such a look of purpose & arrangement; it is a recognisable temple, even now.

We promptly sat down with our backs to the sight we had come to see, & began to eat sandwiches: half an hour afterwards we were ready to make our inspection.

The singular, & intoxicating charm of Stonehenge to me, & to most I think, is that no one in the world can tell you anything about it. There are these great blocks of stone; & what more? Who piled them there & when, & for what purpose, no one in the world – I like to repeat my boast – can tell.

I felt as though I had run against the stark remains of an age I cannot otherwise conceive; a piece of wreckage washed up from Oblivion. There are theories I know – without end; & we, naturally, made a great many fresh, & indisputable discoveries of our own. The most attractive, & I suppose most likely, is that some forgotten people built here a Temple where they worshipped the sun; there is a rugged pillar someway out side the circle whose peak makes exactly that point on the rim of the earth where the sun rises in the summer solstice. And there is a fallen stone in the middle, longer & larger then the other hewn rocks it lies among which may have been an altar – & the moment the sun rose the Priest of that savage people slaughtered his victim here in honour of the Sun God. We certainly saw the dent of his axe in the stone. Set up the pillars though in some other shape, & we have an entirely fresh picture; but the thing that remains in ones mind, whatever one does, is the stupendous mystery of it all. Man has done nothing to change Salisbury plain since these stones were set here; they have seen sunrise & moonrise over those identical swells & ridges for – I know not how many thousand years. I like to think of it; imagine those toiling pagans doing honour to the very sun now in the sky above me, & for some perverse reason I find this a more deeply impressive temple of Religion – block laid to block, & half of them tumbled in ruin so long that the earth almost hides them, than that perfect spire whence prayer & praise is at this very moment ascending.

It is matter for thought surely, if not for irony, that as one stands on the ruins of Stonehenge one can see the spire of Salisbury Cathedral.

It would be a matter for thought, if it were true: but Salisbury Cathedral is invisible from Stonehenge – which has gone through many permutations of degradation since 1903, and in 1992 could be viewed by the public only from a distance.

. . . Our drive took us on to the Downs, & we observed an unusual commotion among the population of flocks. They were all attended by shepherds in their best Sunday clothes – & dogs too, who looked more than usually alert. Some were driven into their pens to feed, others were being hounded out – but the greater part of the flocks were marching along the road, all with their noses turned in the same direction. We met drove after drove, so closely packed in the lane that we wondered how on earth we were to pass. The shepherd whistled his dog, shouted something unintelligible to us, but at once understood by the dog, who clove a passage for us in an incredibly short time.

Every now & then we met a drove of calves – & the secret was out when a terrible puffing ahead, as of a goods train going at foots pace, proclaimed a traction engine. There were two of these monsters. Somebodys Steam Circus, it turned out – & these were followed by a whole caravan of gipsies. Next day was Wilton fair – These gipsies travel the country, from fair to fair, all through the summer. They are, we were told, the genuine breed, talkers of Romany & all the rest, who under pretence of earning a livelihood at fairs like the respectable world, live their own gipsy life, which is otherwise impossible. I never see a gipsy cart without longing to be inside it. A house that is rooted to no one spot but can travel as quickly as you change your mind, & is complete in itself is surely the most desirable of houses. Our modern house with its cumbersome walls & its foundations planted deep in the ground is nothing better than a prison; & more & more prison like does it become the longer we live there & wear fetters of association & sentiment, painful to wear – still more painful to break.

The fair itself is the greatest sheep fair in this part of the Kingdom. It brings the shepherds from their downs – the farmers from their far away farms – & the country folk from all the villages within a days journey. It is thus a remarkable day in the calendar – a day of social meeting as well as of business. You could see here a very curious type of face – that of the shepherd who passes his life with his flocks on the down. He is far more interesting to observe than his sheep. His face is not coarsened; & yet is not the face of a man who has mixed with his fellow men; it is the face of a middle aged man but it has the freshness & simplicity of a childs. The eye is perfectly clear & shrewd; the face is tanned red & brown, & creased with a multitude of fine lines, but it is easy to see that they have come there when the eyes are screwed to observe the weather, or the brow is puckered against the wind – & have nothing whatever to do with any mental perplexity. His best coat is a relic of a more festive age, & is a rich chestnut, or plum colour, grown mellow with years; he wears corduroy breeches, a large felt hat, & he grasps a staff in his hand high up near the top. A more typically English figure I imagine it would be hard to find than this Wiltshire down shepherd.

There are still sheep fairs at Wilton though they are now straightforward auctions, without attendant amusements. There are travelling people about, too, especially at the summer solstice which brings a colourful variety of pilgrims to Stonehenge (or would bring them there, if Authority would permit it).

. . . The notion of seeing the Wilton Carpet factory crossed our minds. Providence, or again that power which takes our education to heart, arranged matters in a surprisingly convenient way – Wednesday it chanced was the one day in the week on which the factory is open to visitors. Wilton is the last place one thinks likely to hold a factory; its air tastes unpolluted by any smoke save that of snug domestic hearths, & its streets are surely the oldest in England. But nevertheless there is a factory – of a kind. It has little likeness I imagine to the factories of Birmingham & Manchester. We entered by a door which looked like the entrance to the stables of an inn, & found ourselves in a courtyard, which again looked very much like the courtyard of an old fashioned posting house. The buildings round it are low & ramshackle; there is no hum of machinery, no bustle of workpeople; I expected to be led on to some further, & more imposing buildings. But instead our guide – a wrinkled old countryman – opened a door on the left: we were in the factory. It was a long low room like one of the long rooms in a mill; down the middle there was suspended a wooden cylinder; round which were stretched the strings which make the foundation of a carpet. Girls were seated on one side of this, twisting coloured threads round the strings with most dexterous fingers; they then beat them down on top of the work already done with a metal comb. Above them was pinned the design of the carpet – but I remain quite unable to understand how they carried this out – as they did without hesitation – or how it resulted in the very elaborate pattern which was woven into the finished work. The benches were by no means crowded; but the girls that were there worked hard enough, & in silence. Their faces were not unhappy; but they had all of them – the youngest was twelve I suppose – the pale preoccupied look of people who sit long hours over hard work, from which their attention can never stray, though the depths of the mind are unstirred. We went through two or three rooms of this kind – all of them low & badly lighted, with no modern machinery or furniture. The look of the whole place indeed was dusty & ramshackle, & obsolete; our guide made it clear to us that this is indeed the case . . . All their work is done by hand . . .

The factory soon went bankrupt, but had a new lease of life in 1905 when the 14th Earl of Pembroke started a new company – in that year it wove a carpet, for the Carlton Club in London, so big that it took twenty-seven porters to move it. It was still working in 1992, though part of it was up for sale: its workroom had been supplemented by a museum and a café. At least one of the looms that Virginia found so old-fashioned in 1903, I was told, continued to weave until 1959.

There is one day – Wednesday – in every week when from the hour of 2 till 5 – the public can enter the great gates of Wilton as freely as any Herbert in the land. I have never been over one of our 'stately homes' in any capacity, so yesterday I thought I would earn that experience. I expected to find a crowd of wagonettes & bicycles – but as a matter of fact I had to enter modestly behind a solitary party of three – an elderly gentleman, who might be a banker in

Salisbury, & his two nieces, who were young ladies from
New York – & signed themselves thus in the visitors book.
This at any rate was my guess at their relationship to each
other; the gentleman was certainly English, for he took
upon himself to do the honours of Wilton, & point out the
qualities of English scenery, as though he were responsible
for both, & had a lawful interest to any credit that might be
laid to their account. A massive lodge keeper in livery
admitted us, took our shilling, for the benefit of the Herbert
Hospital, & forwarded us across the courtyard to the care of
a dignified house keeper within the doors. I felt unspeak-
ably ignominious, as though I were admitted by favour of
these gorgeous flunkeys, & had to hold myself in an attitude of servile attention to them. The good lady who took
charge of us was a typical family servant. She was willing to
gratify our awed curiosity as to the Herbert family & their
belongings – & at the same time she clearly felt herself to be
socially our superior. She did the honours with the condescending air of one to whom Greek statues & Vandykes
are a matter of course, but she expected our plebian respect. So we trooped behind her obediently, & were sub-
missively awe-struck. When she thought I suppose that I
was looking about me with too critical an air she enunciated
in my ear some high sounding title – as 'Portrait of Titian – by
himself' which was to recall me from my impertinence.

There are undoubtedly a great many very good pictures – but a still greater number of worthless ones. I am a
person of no discrimination in matters of art – I dont even
know what I like – at once that is – & the conditions under
which I saw the Wilton pictures were altogether unfavour-
able. Indeed it was difficult to appreciate the house itself
even – ushered as we were from one museum like room to
another, & bade admire the proper things as quickly as possible & pass on to the next.

Honestly, I was disappointed in my first view of a great
house. I had imagined something more spacious & more
harmonious. It was as though they had tried in parts to
make an early Victorian style of decoration harmonise with

the Vandykes – & had not succeeded. If they had resolved to keep the whole place in the style of one period – if the chairs & tables had been uniformly old instead of all styles & ages – the character of the rooms would have been distinct & beautiful. As it is your eye is distracted by a confusion of chintzes & leather chairs & handsome writing tables which are all out of character with the old chimney pieces & moulded walls. – But, having let a week almost, lapse between this sentence & the last, I can find nothing very profitable to say about the beauties of Wilton. The American young ladies I remember, showed a far more spontaneous interest in the photographs & armchairs of the Herbert family than in the famous Vandykes & Titians – though they did their duty manfully by these too. The Banker uncle produced for them the special privilege of holding the present Earls portrait in their hands: & the housekeeper beamed a condescending approval.

She was so condescending indeed that as we stood in the hall, I was terribly un-easy in my mind what course to take with a certain half crown that lay in my hand. Half a crown was lavish payment I felt; but then it was the smallest coin I had; yet when I looked at the ladys face, the good breeding I saw there made my half crown seem paltry – not to say vulgar – I waited, like a coward, for the banker to decide. If he dared, I dared, & the half crown was doomed; but apparently he had no doubts in his mind. He bade her a hearty good day, & thank you – & left without putting his hand in his pocket.

I still have my doubts as to whether the glance that she cast on us as we left, had not appreciably increased in scorn – but I was soon out of range.

Nowadays Wilton is open to the public on most days, and one is no longer obliged to suffer a guided tour. The phrase 'stately homes', used here by Virginia Woolf in inverted commas, was finally put into the general vernacular by Noël Coward in 1938, but had been first used in this context in 1827 by Felicia Hemans, author of 'The boy stood on the burning deck'.

Stratford-upon-Avon

Diary, 9 May 1934

. . . All crabbers be damned – it is a fine un self conscious town, mixed, with 18th Century & the rest all standing cheek by jowl. All the flowers were out in Sh[akespea]re's garden. 'That was where his study windows looked out when he wrote the Tempest' said the man. And perhaps it was true. Anyhow it was a great big house, looking straight at the large windows & the great stone of the school chapel, & when the clock struck, that was the sound Shre heard. I cannot without more labour than my roadrunning mind can compass describe the queer impression of sunny impersonality. Yes, everything seemed to say, this was Shakespeare's, had he sat & walked; but you wont find me not exactly in the flesh. He is serenely absent-present; both at once; radiating round one; yes; in the flowers, in the old hall, in the garden; but never to be pinned down. And we went to the Church, & there was the florid foolish bust, but what I had not reckoned for was the worn simple slab, turned the wrong way, Kind Friend for Jesus' sake forbear – again he seemed to be all air & sun smiling serenely; & yet down there one foot from me lay the little bones that had spread over the world this vast illumination. Yes, & then we

112

walked round the church, & all is simple & a little worn; the river slipping past the stone wall, with a red breadth in it from some flowering tree, & the edge of the turf unspoilt, soft & green & muddy, & two casual nonchalant swans. The church & the school & the house are all roomy spacious places, resonant, sunny today, & in & out . . . – yes, an impressive place; still living, & then the little bones lying there, which have created: to think of writing The Tempest looking out on that garden; what a rage & storm of thought to have gone over any mind; no doubt the solidity of the place was comfortable. No doubt he saw the cellars with serenity. And a few scented American girls, & a good deal of parrot prattle from old gramophone discs at the birthplace, one taking up the story from the other. But isnt it odd, the caretaker at New Place agreed, that only one genuine signature of S.'s is known; & all the rest, books, furniture pictures &c has completely vanished? Now I think Shre was very happy in this, that there was no impediment of fame, but his genius flowed out of him, & is still there, in Stratford. They were acting As you like it I think in the theatre.

Wells

1908

In the summer of 1908 Virginia Woolf and her two dogs, Gurth and Hans, spent two weeks holidaying in the little cathedral city of Wells, Somerset. She lodged first in Vicars Close, a fourteenth-century street of terraces built for minor functionaries of the cathedral.

I live in these lodgings about as near the sacred precincts as possible. Bells toll, & people shuffle down the Close to prayers. It is exactly the place in which some grey superstition should linger; what breath can ever blow down these crooked alleys, all crusted with medieval stone; a print of Wells in the 17th Century is precisely the same as a photograph of Wells in the 19th. But if Christianity is ever tolerable, it is tolerable in these old sanctuaries; partly because age has robbed it of its power, & you can fondle a senile old creature, when you must strike with all your force at [a] young & lusty parson. Nevertheless the young minister to the old; there are theological students everywhere, young men lately come from college, who give up their days to studying its laws, & will give up their lives to expounding them. As a matter of fact they will hunt, & fish,

& live much the same lives as the smaller country gentry. The Cathedral of course dominates the whole place, & Wells without it is no more than a pleasant country town, with the usual number of antiquities: I believe I wrong it though. Certain night walks have shown me battlements & a moat; & there is a stately square, which, when I first saw it, was crowded with farmers, listening in a circle, to the vociferations of a little old man in a cap & gown; he walked round & round his compound, in the middle of which a boy held his standard – a flaring gas jet. He bade the rustics not envy the rich – He had supple lips, & an infinite succession of phrases, though why he used them, I could not tell. Perhaps the peroration was to celebrate some brand of pills, for he did not look a disinterested servant of truth.

Diary, August (undated)

In 1908 Vicars Close was mostly occupied as lodgings by the Wells Theological College. Today it is dominated by Wells Cathedral School, but physically is very much as it was in Virginia's day. The 'stately square' I take to be the modest market-place, now largely occupied by car parks, outside Penniless Porch, the southern gateway to the cathedral precincts.

The Close has filled itself with theological students, & I am not sorry to leave. For they live a healthy life, in & out all day, much conversation, meetings on the stairs, greetings at the gate – till the cheery male voice is as the drone of bluebottles in my ear.

I have moved to a dusky old house in the Green; one of those spacious houses, which are rather shabby & threadbare now, but were built for prosperity. A candle has to burn perpetually in a corner, to illumine the steep stairs; which have bannisters of carved oak & great oaken balls at the landing. A tree, all draped with foliage stands directly in front of the windows, & increases the dimness of the atmosphere within. The Cathedral Green is rather spent by the time it reaches this far corner, & the grass, upon which you may not walk, elsewhere, seems here to lose its sacred character & to become a playground of the children of the neighbouring houses. My house has two children attached to it, & I [am] led to think a good deal about the nature of children. They play all day in front of me. Did I ever play all day when I was a child? I cant remember it. They have no regular games, or hours; but merely tumble about, hit at balls, upset chairs, run into the house & out again, fall & hurt themselves, fly into passions, & talk incessantly. At a certain hour, the smallest child, aged 3, gets tired & runs off to her mother, who puts her to bed; she wakes, & comes out to join the sport again.

Dairy, August (undated)

To this day boys sometimes play football on the Green, the big grass area outside the west doors of the cathedral – perhaps the only cathedral close in England where it would be allowed. Virginia's lodgings during her second week in Wells were with a Mr and Mrs Oram at 5 Cathedral Green, on the north side; but so confusing is the numeration of the Green, so often has it been changed since 1908, and so conflicting are the helpful suggestions of today's residents, that for the life of me I have been unable to identify the house.

When I got home I was solemnly waited on by Mr Oram, who begged me not to be agitated . . . The slavy had taken the dogs for a walk, they had escaped; they had 'cruised about the town', till a policeman found them, and put them in prison, finding that Gurth had no address on his collar.

Mr Oram had fetched them back; but the policeman wished to see me. All this he repeated over and over again, adding his theory: that 'Miss Hans had run away, and his Lordship (Gurth) followed after. O she's a sprightly little lady. But dont be agitated ma'am: my advice to you is this; say that the address is now being engraved. I would not recommend anybody to trifle with their conscience in an ordinary way, but a young lady, travelling alone – its very awkward. Do not consider, ma'am, that you are, in the eye of the law, a criminal . . .'

I met the policeman this morning, as I took Gurth to the station, and he merely suggested that some day I had better get a new collar . . . Hans has just been violently sick.

Letter to Vanessa Bell, 14 August

Gazetteer

Bath

🐦 We . . . strolled around the Circus where a band of white haired gentlemen played selections from Gluck and Handel. Once I clapped, and all the eye-glasses were raised in astonishment. The fashion paraded past us, at a foots pace.

Letter to Saxon Sydney-Turner, 10 August 1908

🐦 Bath: quite magnificent. Every street like Pope or Dryden: and everywhere Burke stayed or Sir Walter Scott, Wordsworth and Fanny Burney. I can't see why it isnt more famous than Cambridge and Oxford together.

Letter to Vita Sackville-West, 5 May 1930

Some two million visitors went to Bath in 1992, and the Roman Baths there were the third most popular paid tourist attraction in England, after the Tower of London and Westminster Abbey.

Brighton

🐦 We went for a treat to Brighton; and had a delightful time – wandering into back streets full of most improper little shops, and past the great bow windows, where the old ladies and their pets were sunning themselves.

Letter to Lady Robert Cecil, 25 October 1915

At Fuller's [teashop]. A fat, smart woman, in red hunting cap, pearls, check skirt, consuming rich cakes. Her shabby dependant also stuffing . . . The fat woman had a louche large white muffin face. T'other was slightly grilled. They ate & ate . . . Something scented, shoddy, parasitic about them . . . Where does the money come to feed these fat white slugs? Brighton a love corner for slugs. The powdered the pampered the mildly improper.

Diary, 26 February 1941

Bristol

I can't describe the horror of Bristol on Friday – 200 stout burgesses, crammed and dripping, and having to talk about art after losing my way in the most hideous of all towns.

Letter to Lady Ottoline Morrell, 14 July 1935

Within five years much of Bristol's centre would be destroyed by bombing, to be replaced for the most part by buildings a good deal worse.

Cheddar

A wretched place, like the scenery beside a switch back, crowded, and full of grottoes and caves, into which I could not bother to look.

Letter to Vanessa Bell, 14 August 1908

The Cotswolds

All today we spent driving around the Cotswolds, which

were about as beautiful, or is it my eyes are going? – as the Campagna. Really, the country was astonishing, and all the villages made of yellow stone, and not a new house any-where. We went 40 miles to see a necromancer – that is a retired East Indian planter who lives in a mediaeval farm which he has filled with old clothes, bicycles, mummies, alligators, Italian altars – not, I thought, very interesting.

Letter to Vanessa Bell, 3 July 1935

The 'necromancer', Charles Wade (1883-1956), whose money came from the West rather than the East Indies, lived at Snowshill Manor, near Broadway, where his magpie collection is now looked after by the National Trust.

Derbyshire

Bald moors, the strangest looking places. So solitary they might be 18th century England, the valleys cut by a thread of water falling roughly from heights; great sweeps of country all sunny & gloomy with bare rocks against the sky, & then behold a row of east end slum houses, with a strip of pavement & two factory chimneys set down in the midst. The houses are all stone, bleak, soot stained ... now and again no houses but wild moors, a thread of road, & farms set into the earth, uncompromising, since nothing like flowers, long grass, or hedges grow around them. 'Yes', I said to Mrs Unwin, 'Derbyshire is a very fine county'.

Diary, 18 March 1921

Dorset

Cranbourne Chase: the stunted aboriginal forest trees, scattered, not grouped in cultivations; anemones, bluebells, violets, all pale, sprinkled about, without colour, livid, for the sun hardly shone. Then Blackmore Vale; a vast air dome & the fields dropped to the bottom; the sun striking, there, there; a drench of rain falling, like a veil streaming from the sky, there & there; & the downs rising, very strongly scarped . . . so that they were ridged & ledged . . . & then tea & cream . . . & the drive to Bournemouth, & the dog & the lady behind the rock, & the view of Swanage, & coming home.

Diary, 18 April 1926

Glastonbury

 [The ruins] are too clean, and too dilapidated; besides new scaffolding is all over them, and there are benches at the proper views, notices about the sacred building; and middle class bicyclists resting their ugly bodies all over the place.

Letter to Vanessa Bell, 4 August 1908

Manchester

 All Manchester streets are the same, & all strung with tramlines . . . You hear bells striking all the time. Then there are no great shops, but great cafes; & no little shops, but all big drapers . . . None of this was quite English, or at least London. The people were lower middle class, no sprinkling of upper class.

Diary, 18 March 1921

 The Manchester Zoo . . . you must admit it was exciting to find a dromedary and an Indian buffaloe, with ingrowing toenails, poor beast, in a grotto of pale grey stone, totally forgotten, there being only 2 charwomen about the place, which is the size of Regents Park, and almost entirely given over to the scaffolding of a panorama, and a lake. But how I love these places! The whole expedition is one long rapture of romance.

Letter to Vanessa Bell, 17 March 1921

In 1921 the Manchester Zoo (Belle Vue) was a family concern, run by the descendants of its nineteenth-century founder John Jennison: besides its own railway station, it had an associated brewery and a gasworks.

Oxfordshire

In this country everything is made of silvery grey flaky stone, & the houses cluster round, with their little gables, all crowded, ancient, with roses, with haystacks, & the river [Thames] flowing in the great grass meadows, all untouched, beyond the builders ring, which begins at Abingdon, & then till London all becomes red brick Georgian; & Riverine, that is gramophontic, girls in trousers, young men in shorts, and noisy & strident.

Diary, 15 July 1935

Hadrian's Wall

We were 2 days on the wall: lay on top of it the one hot day; and saw the landscape that to me is the loveliest in the world; miles and miles of lavender coloured loneliness, with one thread white path; dear me, were I a writer, how I could describe that: the immensity and tragedy and the sense of the Romans, and time, and eternity; and then the wild white hawthorn, and the sheep cropping, and 3 little white headed boys playing in a Roman camp.

Letter to Ethel Smyth, 26 June 1938

Salisbury Plain

The finest thing in England is Salisbury Plain, or was, until your cursed army peppered it with huts and bugle calls. How the druids must hate the Colonels!

Letter to Ethel Smyth, 27 April 1934

Somerset

It is a wide land, uneasy, like the sea, full of mounds, & high lines into the horizon. When the sun gleamed, great bones of green & brown earth showed in the middle of this scene, which was coloured like some drawing in brown ink. The kingdoms of the world lay before me, a rich domain, teeming in the folds with apples, & meadows, with gray villages snug in hollows, & little steeples. Far away the sea, into which the land may spill its treasure.

Diary, August 1908 (undated)

Weymouth

I rather think Weymouth is the most beautiful seaside town in Europe, combining the grace of Naples with the sobriety of George the Third.

Letter to Vanessa Bell, 11 May 1936

Anglicisms

The Look of England

 When we landed, the English coast seemed long low sweeping empty. I exclaimed at the extraordinary English green – with its silver mixture; & L. said the earth had an unbaked look – no red in it; & the lines of the hills so sloping. Now our road seems a garden path.

Diary, May 1932, on returning from Greece

The Age of England

 The antiquity of England is inconceivable. What is to be done about it? . . . Have you ever conceived the antiquity of England in a thousand years? – Every Inn we stay at has been an inn since the time of Arthur or Alfred.

Letter to Vita Sackville-West, May 1930

English Hotels

 A vast green plush room – pillars – candelabra – silver trays – urns – coffee pots – large British family groups reading newspapers – drinking – the clergy – mothers and daughters – all grey tidy skimpy incredibly respectable – save for one or two hippotamus females basking in corners all stuck about with diamonds – and old gentlemen bursting through their waistcoats – indeed they never stop eating fried fish, tea, and meringues.

Letter to Vanessa Bell, about Queen's Hotel, Manchester, 17 March 1921

How I yawn! The evenings are the worst – nowhere to sit; or a room full of old, suspicious widow ladies, whispering to each other. Not an Inn from London here is without its six or seven. And once they were married, and once they had children. And my head spins wondering what they're doing in Truro tonight.

Letter to Ethel Smyth, about a hotel in Truro, 6 May 1930

Bells dont ring; hot water cold; but still a great air of the 18th century in the coffee room, where we sit before a huge fire, with the clergy and the travellers in biscuits.

Letter to Vita Sackville-West, about the King's Arms Hotel, Launceston,
8 May 1930

Stayed at the best hotel in Lyme [Regis], in which the very pots were seasoned with camphor . . . I don't see how civilization can be splitting when theres not an arm chair without its old couple and all so urbane and kind.

Letter to Vanessa Bell, 11 May 1936

The only people in the hotel were purple-faced majors from Hong Kong, and rather dishevelled, slightly vinous ladies, who told the stories of their private lives in loud voices, to my delight. One of their husbands had committed suicide.

Letter to Katherine Arnold-Foster, about a hotel at Coverack, Cornwall,
21 May 1936

I could write at least 16 reams about life in the hotel here. There was an otter hunting party at breakfast this morning

... Old ladies of 70 appeared in tweed suits with the pads of otters or foxes mounted in gold pinned to their breasts. Last night I was shut up alone with two spinsters; who after welcoming very kindly, turned upon each other with such ferocity that the room rang. All reticence was forgotten. Their skirts rose over their long brown legs. And now they're reading opposite.

Letter to Vanessa Bell, 18 June 1938, about the George Inn, Chollerford, Northumberland

Isn't the Mermaid [Inn, at Rye] rather dismal – like a battleship in the time of Nelson – I remember creeping into it one day, and an old woman chased me out.

Letter to Lytton Strachey, 4 January 1909

Summer Day

What a day it was – the sea flowing in & out of the bays, all the way, like the Adriatic, or Pacific; & the sand yellow; & the boats steaming along; & behind the downs like long waves, gently extending themselves, to break very quickly; smooth & sloping like the waves. Even bungalows are all burnt up & made part of this beauty; made of vapour not zinc.

Diary, 31 May 1929, after a visit to Worthing, Sussex

Hunting

Mystery of sound reaching one through the trees; the distant music of hounds running. The note of the huntsmans horn, & far away voices of men shouting, all sound as in some distant romantic dream; as though falling through an ocean of waters.

Diary, Hampshire, Christmas 1904

An English Eclipse

We crept up to the top of Bardon Fell [Barden Fell, York-shire, to see a total eclipse of the sun]. Here were people camping beside their cars. We got out, & found ourselves very high, on a moor, boggy, heathery, with butts for grouse shooting ... One light burnt down there. Vales & moors stretched, slope after slope ... Four great red setters came leaping over the moor. There were sheep feeding behind us ... I thought how we were very like old people, in the birth of the world – druids on Stonehenge ... Rapidly, very very quickly, all the colours faded; it became darker & darker as at the beginning of a violent storm; the light sank & sank ... Suddenly the light went out. We had fallen. It was extinct. There was no colour. The earth was dead.

Diary, 30 June 1927

A Fortnight in Kent

The rain falls, & the birds never give over singing, & hot sulphur fumes rise from the valleys, & the red cow in the field roars for her calf ... We sit exposed to wind & wet by day; & by night, we are invaded by flocks of white moths. They frizzle in the candles, & crawl up my skirt to die, in the hollow of my knee.

Letter to Saxon Sydney-Turner, 13 June 1910

A Visit to Gloucestershire

Rained most of the day. In the afternoon we went out for a most grizzly walk.

Diary, 26 August 1897

Rained. We went out somewhere I think; but I quite forget.

Diary, 27 August 1897

January in London

By God – I mean never to spend February, March, April in London again. Rome, Munich, Moscow – anywhere anywhere out of this damp, dull, dripping dustpan.

Letter to Clive Bell, 31 January 1928

English People

We had the Curate [of Warboys, Cambridgeshire] to dinner last night . . . This young man seems to be largely a person of intelligence with a rather peculiar gift of humorous sarcasm . . . the first 5 minutes of his talk with us he declared that the only thing that made life in the country bearable was rabbit shooting.

Diary, 10 August 1899

I met an old man on the [Lyndhurst, Hampshire] village green yesterday who told me he had had goose for dinner and 'really thought he was the happiest old man in the world'. He looked so convinced of it and so stealthy as though happiness was not altogether respectable that I told him he was a credit to the race and upon wh. he shambled off to the public house, and I nearly followed.

Letter to Violet Dickinson, 28 (?) December 1906

This morning [at Playden, Sussex] the sound of a scythe sharpened proclaimed that it was the gardeners day. He . . . stands six foot, but his prodigious stoop must waste at least ten inches. All day long he has been swinging his scythe across the lawn, so regularly that you might fancy him a figure moved by clockwork . . . When I went to pick roses, & complimented him on the fineness of the crop, he bent willingly, all tremulous & bedewed with his toil. His eyes had pale rings round the pupils as you have seen in the eye of some vague old dog.

Diary, September 1907 (undated)

◗We are in an Inn full of north country people, who are very grim to look at, but so up to date that one blushes with shame. They discuss Thomson's poetry, and post impressionism, and have read everything, and at the same time control all the trade in Hides, and can sing comic songs and do music hall turns – in fact the Bloomsbury group was stunted in the chrysalis compared with them.

Letter to Katherine Cox, from the Cottage Hotel, Wooler,
(now the Tankerville Arms, home of the Tankyburger), 12 August 1914

◗On Easter Monday we went to ... Hampstead Heath. Our verdict was that the crowd at close quarters is detestable; it smells; it sticks; it has neither vitality nor colour; it is a tepid mass of flesh scarcely organized into human life. How slow they walk! How passively & brutishly they lie on the grass! How little of pleasure or pain is in them!

Diary, 24 April 1919

◗'Palaeolithic men must have lived here. They lived an extraordinary kind of life', we agreed in Asheham Hollow [Sussex]. 'Now & then the clever ones realized they were human'.

Diary, 5 September 1923

◗She [a lady of Rodmell, Sussex] had a (face) nose like the Duke of Wellington & great horse teeth & cold prominent eyes. When we came in she was sitting perched on a 3 cornered chair with knitting in her hands. An arrow fastened her collar. And before 5 minutes had passed she had told us that two of her sons had been killed in the war. This, one felt, was to her credit ... Everything in the room was red brown & glossy. Sitting there I tried to coin a few compliments. But they perished in the icy sea between us. And then there was nothing.

Diary, 24 March 1941

This was in Virginia's last diary entry. She died four days later.

Away

Away from home, in Virginia Woolf's life, was never away for long. She was never out of England for more than seven weeks, her most protracted absence being a trip to Greece and Turkey in 1906. Most of her journeys were for a week or ten days. In the course of her life she visited eleven other countries, if only for a day or two, but she wrote about most of them only in diaries or snatches of correspondence, and sometimes her ecstasy was balanced by her homesickness.

Wales

Virginia Woolf's earliest surviving writings about an un-English place are about Wales, and concern the village of Manorbier in what was then Pembrokeshire (now Dyfed). She went there twice, the first time with members of her family after the death of her father in 1904.

We have come to the right place . . . I haven't seen such splendid wild country since St. Ives [Cornwall] – indeed one thinks of St. Ives in many ways. We have already spent an astonishing amount of time walking about on the cliffs. Even lying in the sun. We live almost under the shadow of a great feudal castle, which stands on a cliff over the sea . . .

There are about 3 houses here, and a wild queer Church on the hill. It is cold, but very clear and bright, and no sound but wind and sea.

Letter to Violet Dickinson, 28 February 1904

Eighteen years later Virginia recalled, in her diary entry for 3 September 1922, that during this stay in Manorbier she first realised her vocation as a writer. 'I was for knowing all that was to be known, and for writing a book – a book – but what book? That vision came to me more clearly at Manorbier . . . walking the down on the edge of the sea.'

In 1908 she returned to Manorbier, alone this time, taking lodgings in a cottage called Sea View, 'with a great bow window facing the sea, several deep arm chairs, and a desk'. The weather was extremely variable, and she called it a good country for toads.

It is a lean country, scarcely inhabited, & the one church which does duty for many miles, is a threadbare place, a grey barn some 5 centuries old, to which a tower has been added at one end. The little bay however, is guarded by an immense mass of ruin, the Castle; it is still foursquare, &, it is dark – you see a red glow in some of the slits & openings, which tells that some one finds it still stout enough to live in. Why anyone found it necessary to build such a fortress here, I cannot remember; & at present the character of the land seems markedly worn & poverty stricken, as though it could not support such a monster; or perhaps lay cowed beneath its feet. However this may be, I like my view of it . . . In the evening I walk down to the beach, which I have to myself, & pace a turn or two beside the sea. I like to turn back from looking out along the uneasy & melancholy gray surface, to find a beautiful reflection of it in the gray ruin, & the green & gray sand hills, sprinkled with sheep, which is just colonised by a dozen sky gray cottages. No one will ever make this a watering place, I prophesy; it wants somehow the boldness & self confidence to be a success. I have not walked far, but my investigations tend to show that there is something a little weak in the coast. It is just too low, or too sharp to be impressive. The land within swells into long breakers. I walked through a little village the other day, which seemed to me as deserted as any I had seen. There were cottages splashed with cream coloured wash, out of which came bent old women, of tremendous age; their faces were all white ridges, without any spirit left. Ah, the loneliness of these little distant places! I saw that the pillar box was all discoloured; & there was only one house that tried to be a house – to wear the distinct dress. It had some odd ornament of piled stones in the gateways.

I come down from my room . . . at about half past nine,

blowing out my lamp, & leaving my books. Sometimes it is quite calm, & gray outside; but tonight I was fairly whirled round by the wind & the rain. The only guide I had was the crunch of gravel beneath my feet – I could neither see nor hear. Suppose a cart advanced I should embrace the horse before I saw him. However I had but 200 yards to walk, & by moving my legs automatically, I became aware of a shape like the keel of a large boat on one side of me, & the faint refulgence of window. Still other people are on the roads, leading their horses, or driven to turn in at wayside cottages – The wind is really high; it is sensible peace to sit as I do, behind a pane of glass, with a glaring lamp beside me; even so, gusts get at my candle. I can't read at ease, for the wind is always leaping on to its own back. I hear water too, & the fluttering of a little bush beside my window. Think of the earth given up to this power tonight!

Diary, August 1908 (undated)

Manorbier Castle was founded in the twelfth century, as only an Englishwoman would not realise, to sustain Norman supremacy among the Welsh. It is chiefly famous in Wales as the birthplace of the medieval historian Giraldus Cambrensis, Gerallt Cymro, and parts of it are still inhabited (when I was there in 1992 a Jehovah's Witness wedding reception was being held in the inner ward). Virginia was right – Manorbier never has become an important watering-place, and remains charmingly modest, though not so deserted, lonely and geriatric as it seems to have been in 1908. Sea View has been renamed, and there is some dissent about which house it is, but I believe it to be Awelon ('Breezes'), which stands beside the hill to the north of the village, was occupied in 1992 by kind Welsh-speaking people, and has a grand view of the castle.

Scotland

1938

Like most English upper-class families the Stephens liked to recall that they had Scottish blood in them. In 1927 Virginia Woolf gave her novel To the Lighthouse *a vaguely Hebridean setting, but she did not set eyes on the country until 1938, when she and Leonard Woolf drove through the Highlands to visit the Western Isles. Even then the journey was abandoned because it rained so much.*

...We drove through the Highlands, and there was one lake, with trees reflected which I think carried beauty to the extreme point: whether its expressible, that rapture, I doubt: green and purple trees hanging upside down in the middle of a perfectly still lake, and green all round.

Letter to Ethel Smyth, 26 June

We are now in Oban, which is, as far as I have seen it, the Ramsgate of the Highlands. Only the Scotch having melancholy in their bones – thats where The Stephen's, as Julian said, get their black melancholy, turned to madness in some of us by a drop of French blood, – being entirely without frivolity build even bathing sheds of granite let alone hotels. The result is grim; and on every lamp post is a notice, Please do not spit on the pavement. We had a terrific drive yesterday in one of the worst known gales, over the wildest passes. Trees were hurtling; rivers simply cataractuous, but very beautiful, if the rain had stopped; but it didnt. Our petrol gave out; and the oil clogged the engine. But miracles happen, and suddenly an Inn appeared, in a black gorge; and on opening the door, there were 20 tables with cloths laid diamond shape, maids in white aprons, and 7 different cakes; including the best shortbread I've ever eaten. We were warmly welcomed by the 20 old fishing men and women – they're practically sexless, and I've often taken one for a dog and vice versa: Some had been fishing in the rain for days and caught one trout. They talk such a brogue I had to invent replies, so off the point that at one moment I was talking about the Queens mother's death [Lady Strathmore] and they were talking about the rarity of polecats or somesuch topic. Then a garage mended the car. off we swept into the desert, and just as night was falling – that is a kind of cadaverous dawn, for the sun neither rises nor sets in the highlands – I saw 2 great deer, bounding from rock to rock . . .

Letter to Vanessa Bell, 28 June

Oban is not in the least grim now – is in fact one of the most cheerful of Scottish towns – but when I asked in 1992 after the hotel that Virginia Woolf had stayed at, the Park, I was told it had fallen down.

In the 1930s the Loch Ness Monster first became a subject of popular discussion – Bertram Mills' Circus was offering a £20,000 reward for its live capture – and the recent drowning in the loch of a rich Englishwoman, Winifred Hambro, had further fired speculation.

We met a charming Irish couple in an Inn, who were in

touch, through friends, with The Monster. They had seen
him. He is like several broken telegraph posts and swims at
immense speed. He has no head. He is constantly seen.
Well, after Mrs Hambro was drowned, the Insurance Company sent divers after her, as she was wearing 30,000
pounds of pearls on her head. They dived and came to the
mouth of a vast cavern, from which hot water poured; and
the current was so strong, and the horror they felt so great,
they refused to go further, being convinced The Monster
lived there, in a hollow under the hill. In short, Mrs Hambro was swallowed. No drowned body is ever recovered
and now the natives refuse to boat or to bathe.

Letter to Vanessa Bell, 25 June

Not a turnip grows [in the Highlands], nor cabbage: but
wild roses, and foxgloves; and though the weather is like a
weathercock, one day is always fine for half the time, and
then freezing. The food varies. Last night even you would
have been tolerably content; simple and indigenous; fish is
the trump card, Leonard says – haddock and herring
divine, but I dont think fish a good invention any time.
Then cakes. Leonard says they are unmatched; I dont like
scones for breakfast, or ginger in the cake. Still the more
frivolous sugar cakes are very good. And the porridge is a
dream. Only I loathe porridge. Theres a good earthy soup –
all vegetables unsorted. That I like, and the splendour of
sausage, bacon, ham, eggs, grapefruit, oatcake, grilled ham
for breakfast – The people are enchanting. Mr Cunningham
the baker is sending me 6 tins of his own shortbread.

Letter to Vanessa Bell, 28 June

Well, here we are in Skye, and it feels like the South Seas –
completely remote, surrounded by sea, people speaking
Gaelic, no railways, no London papers, hardly any inhabitants. Believe it or not, it is (in its way, as people say), so far
as I can judge on a level with Italy, Greece or Florence . . .

One should be a painter. As a writer, I feel the beauty, which is almost entirely colour, very subtle, very change-able, running over my pen, as if you poured a large jug of champagne over a hairpin.

Letter to Vanessa Bell, 25 June

Skye is often raining, but also fine; hardly embodied; semi-transparent; like living in a jelly fish lit up with green light. Remote as Samoa; deserted; prehistoric.

Postcard to Duncan Grant, 27 June

The Woolfs were staying at the Flodigarry Hotel in Portree, née MacNab's Inn, now the Royal. Much of it has been burnt down since their time, and rebuilt in a far from prehistoric manner, with a bistro. The Gaelic language still bravely survives in Skye, and the railway never did get there, but in 1992 work was starting on a bridge, across the narrow Kyle of Lochalsh, which will make it in effect an island no longer.

We've driven round the island [Skye] today, seen Dunge-van, encountered the children of the 27th Chieftain, nice red headed brats: the Castle door being open I walked in; they very politely told me the Castle was shut to visitors, but I could see the gardens. Here I found a gamekeepers larder with the tails of two wild cats. Eagles are said to abound and often carry off sheep: sheep and Skye Terriers are the only industries; the old women live in round huts exactly the shape of skye terriers; and you can count all the natives on 20 feet: but they are very rapacious in the towns, and its no use trying to buy anything, as the price, even of Sally's meat, is at least 6 times higher than in our honest land. All the same, the Scotch are great charmers, and sing through their noses like musical tea kettles.

Virginia meant Dunvegan, the seat of the chiefs of the MacLeod clan, who live there still. It is now generally open to the public.

The 'nice red headed brats' were actually the grandsons of the 28th chieftain, Dame Flora MacLeod; twenty-eight years later, peering over a garden wall in a Chicago suburb, I saw the pair of them parading up and down a lawn playing the bagpipes to loyal American members of their clan. One of them is now the 29th chieftain. Wild cats are scarce on Skye now, Skye Terriers too, but eagles are still about.

There are hints in To the Lighthouse *that the novel was meant to be set in Skye, but Virginia had long known that its background was not very convincingly Hebridean. 'I don't defend my accuracy,' she had written in 1927, in response to a critic who had pointed out that there were no rooks, elms or dahlias in the Western Isles.*

Ireland

1934

Virginia Woolf only once went to Ireland, on a holiday with her husband Leonard in the summer of 1934. The Irish Free State, the future Republic of Ireland, had then been in existence for twelve years. Eamon de Valera was its Taoiseach or Prime Minister, and the former governing class of Anglo-Irish Protestants was in dispirited retreat.

A mixture of Greece, Italy & Cornwall; great loneliness; poverty and dreary villages like squares cut out of West Kensington. Not a single villa or house a-building; great stretches of virgin sea shore; the original land that Cornwall and much of England was in Elizabethan times. And a sense that life is receding. At Lismore [County Waterford] the Tchekov innkeeper said Theyre all going away & leaving their houses; nothing's kept up since the war. So the old man on the island [Garnish, off Glengariff] said today — the very sad gentle old man who longed to talk . . . and crooned & moaned leaning on the rake with which he was heaping up some kind of weed. Yes there is a great melancholy in a deserted land, though the beauty remains untouched.

Diary, 30 April

The Woolfs were nevertheless so attracted by Glengariff, County Cork, that they thought of buying a house there. The sad old man who longed to talk was one of the O'Sullivan brothers, who looked after the spectacular gardens of Garnish Island, then privately owned: Garnish belongs to the State now, but five or six O'Sullivans still work as gardeners there, and in 1992 the octogenarian Mrs Maggie O'Sullivan was the only person living on the island.

One of the Woolfs' chief destinations was Bowen's Court, the home of the writer Elizabeth Bowen at Farahy near Kildorrery in County Cork.

... One can see after Bowen's Court, how ramshackle & half squalid the Irish life is, how empty & poverty stricken. There we spent one night ... & it was all as it should be – pompous & pretentious & imitative & ruined – a great barrack of grey stone, 4 storeys & basements, like a town house, high empty rooms, & a scattering of Italian plasterwork, marble mantelpieces, inlaid with brass & so on. All the furniture clumsy solid cut out of single wood – the wake sofa, on wh. the dead lay – carpets shrunk in the great rooms, tattered farm girls waiting, the old man of 90 in his cabin who wdn't let us go – E[lizabe]th had to say Yes The Ladies are very well several times. And we went to the wishing well, where there are broken cups as offerings & half a rosary ... & then I talked to the cook, & she showed me the wheel for blowing the fire in the windy pompous kitchen, half underground ... there was a fine turkey but everywhere desolation & pretention cracked grand pianos, faked old portraits, stained walls – & yet with character & charm, looking on to a meadow where the trees stand in a ring called Lamb's Cradle.

Diary, 30 April

Elizabeth Bowen, who lived until 1973, sold Bowen's Court in 1959, and it was demolished by its new owner. However fragments of the servants' quarters remain, and surrounded by brambles and shrubberies, frequented by rooks, attended by the remains of the great walled garden, make a very evocative ruin. In 1992 a former cook to Elizabeth Bowen, Mrs Molly O'Brien, still lived in Farahy, opposite the former back lodge to the house. St Geoffrey's Well, she told me, though its waters had been immemorially thought beneficial to eye diseases, had fallen into disuse and was hard to reach. No relatives of Patsy Hennessy, the 'old man of 90', remained. The trees called Lambs' Cradle had been cut down – they used to have, she said, 'very velvety leaves'. Mrs O'Brien had not revisited the site for years – ''tis too sad for me, we had such good times up there night and day . . . ' It occurs to me that Virginia Woolf, who evidently did not much like the place, was either envious of its undeniably seigneurial atmosphere, or too urban for its rural austerities.

. . . An extremely interesting encounter at the windy hotel with Ireland – that is Mr & Mrs Rowlands; he is a giant, very shapely, small head, obliterated features; she small, abrupt, vivacious. They began directly, & so we talked, – they accepted us as their sort, & were gentry, Irish gentry, very much so, he with a house 500 years old, & no land left. 'But I love my King & Country. Whatever they ask me to do I'd do it' – this with great emotion. Oh yes, we believe in the British Empire; we hate the madman de Valéra.' There they live, 14 miles from Cork, hunting, with an old retriever dog, & go to bazaars miles & miles away. 'Thats the way we live – no nonsense about us – not like the English people. Now I'll give you my name, & I'll write to my friend & she'll tell you of a house – & I hope you'll live in Ireland. We want people like ourselves. But wait, till the budget.' This she said, with all the airs of the Irish gentry: something very foreign about her . . . & yet in slave to London; of course everyone wants to be English. We think Englands talking of us – not a bit. No said the obliterated Greek torso, for such he was, when I was courting my wife – she lived in Liverpool – the young chaps used to say 'now Paddy tell us one of your stories' but now they dont take any interest in us. But I'd do anything for my King & Country, though you've always treated us very badly . . .

Yes I felt this is the animal that lives in the shell. These are the ways they live – he hunting all day, & she bustling about in her old car, & everybody knowing everybody & laughing & talking & picnicking, & great poverty & some tradition of gentle birth, & all the sons going away to make their livings & the old people sitting there hating the Irish Free State & recalling Dublin & the Viceroy.

Diary, 2 May

I wd like to describe the perfection of Irish conversation, which was Mrs FitzGerald's last night. She is exactly the great French lady – only living in a black jersey on an Irish bog. After dinner she came in, ostensibly to lend us a paper & offer advice, in fact to indulge her genius for talk. She talked till 11, & wd. willingly be talking now: about hotel keeping, about frigidaires, about her grandmother sitting on a chair in the kitchen & saying Thats done that wants another 2 minutes & so on, never stirring herself but somehow getting it done. We have the name of being good housekeepers. Then on about bogs, she has bought several fragments because now there may be money in it. However I can give no notion of the flowing, yet formed sentences, the richness & ease of the language; the lay out, dexterity & adroitness of the arrangement. There was the story of old Julia the cook, who had gone off home in a huff jealous of the young maids; had her daughter & the London husband on her, bought them gramophone records, & now wont own that she has wasted her savings. Mrs F. is one of those bluntnosed parted haired Irishwomen with luminous brown eyes & something sardonic & secretive in her expression. Talk is to her an intoxicant, but there is as Mr Rowlands said, something heartless about the I[rish]: quite cold indifferent sarcastic, for all their melody, their fluency, their adorable ease & forthcomingness. She was very much

on the spot, accurate, managing, shrewd, hardheaded, ana-
lytic. Why arent these people the greatest novelists in the
world? – with this facility, this balance, this fundamental
(now L. has joined in & is advising the 3 ladies. Are they
American?)

Its very kind of you telling us: thank you very much.
Now the wireless is brawling. Everything looks nice in fine
weather. I think I'll go to bed. I want you to read this. One
is the director of the others, severe, but apologetic, perhaps
paid for.

But why isn't Mrs F. a great novelist? Certainly the
salon survives at Glenbeith, the lust for talk, & finishing
one's sentence – only with complete naturalness. For instance, explaining the bogs, 'saturated, now whats the
opposite word?' Desiccated, L. suggested, & she adopted it
with pleasure. She said one could never understand the
Irish: one had to live as they did. They sit in their cottages
talking about politics; they dont dance much; they have no
amusements. They at once started to poach on her bog
merely because she had bought it – otherwise it had been
left alone for centuries. The bogs are full of trees, cant be
self planted, so orderly, but now who has planted them?
And they burn in a resinous way – go up – puf! – in a flash,
like petrol. Suddenly she became severe & thought me a
fool. 'What does this good lady mean?' Her grandmother
was an innkeeper; she herself went away for 25 years; Oh,
as my grandmother said, one becomes able to read peoples
characters before they step over the door, & ones never
wrong one way or the other. Her quickness was amazing.
This morning the talk began & L. very slightly put out his
hand. 'Oh I know that means you wanting to be off' – & so
we parted from the last representative of the French salon
of the 18th Century, this strange mixture of county lady,
peasant, & landlady.

Diary, 3 May

*Mrs Ida Fitzgerald was the proprietress of the Glenbeigh Hotel,
County Kerry, and is well remembered there: the testimonial still*

quoted in the hotel brochure – 'One of the most delightful hotels in the world, owned and run by people of quite extraordinary charm, even by Irish standards' – refers in fact to her regime. Her successor at the hotel, Mrs Mary Keary, who runs it quite as agreeably with the help of her eight children, told me in 1992 that Mrs Fitzgerald was, for all her gifts, far better at talking to women than to men.

A phrase made this windy day: the clouds looping up their skirts & letting down a shaft of light. We picked bright blue gentians on the cliff looking towards the Aran Islands. This, though raining & cloudy, was one of our best drives – to the sea; views over folds of wild land with one or two orange & yellow white cottages: the sea blue, stone coloured or deep black: the waves tossing their hair back. People gathering sea weed & heaping carts. Extreme poverty.

So on to Galway which has 2 great bookshops, otherwise wild, poor, sordid. We saw the Claddagh; shawled women, coated men, all standing in groups together beside thatched huts, like islanders, waiting for a funeral. This the original Irish quarter; G. Thompson whom we found sitting before his Greek books in a little room looking on the sea came to the hotel after dinner & told us how they spend their lives in talk, dont mind poverty so much. He teaches 6 [?] Galways Greek in Irish.

Diary, 4 May

Galway City is nowadays perhaps the liveliest city in all Ireland, and a great place for bookshops still. The Claddagh was a unique Gaelic-speaking fishing quarter of thatched cottages, with its own costumes and its own elected King; it was demolished in the 1930s, and is now just another housing estate, although in 1992 its best-known resident, the octogenarian entertainer Molly Browne, performed a soft-shoe shuffle for me in her front room after a rendition of her best-known number, 'The Laughing Policeman'. George Thompson was a lecturer in Ancient Classics at University College, where the Irish language is still extensively used; the

145

Woolfs entertained him after dinner at the Great Southern Hotel,
still one of the best in town.

The Woolfs finished their tour in Dublin, staying at the now
defunct Russell Hotel on St Stephen's Green, and made a pilgrim-
age to the Protestant Cathedral of St Patrick's to see Dean Swift's
tomb beneath its famous epitaph – 'UBI SAEVA INDIGNATIO
ULTERIUS COR LACERARE NEQUIT' *('Where Savage Indignation*
Can No Longer Tear The Heart').

. . . Over the door are the tremendous words; & in front of
the door a diamond shaped brass, to mark the dean's tomb.
There beside him till a few years ago slept Stella; but the
late Bishop, as the verger sarcastically remarked, pointing
to his name opprobriously on the long list, decided that she
was buried at some distance, & so moved her brass plate. I
suspect this was prudery; & if Swift was buried in her grave,
that seems to amount to marriage. Also her epitaph which
he wrote, alludes to her being celebrated by him. However
the Bishop moved them – & in prudery also Lord Guiness
has cased all the old pillars of Irish marble in stucco, so that
they look like South Kensington, & somebody else, of equal
piety, has floored the whole building with black & red tiles
such as there are in hotels – much to the dudgeon of the old
verger, who, like everybody else, regretted the old days:
showed us the stalls of the Knights of St Patrick, with their
helmets & arms, one the Prince of Wales's another the
Duke of Connaught's 'but they dont come here now' . . .

Diary, 8 May

It was not a Bishop, but Dean Hugh Lawlor, who removed from
Swift's tomb the brass commemorating his beloved Stella. She was
probably not buried there anyway, and the brass had been the gift
of Sir Benjamin Guinness, of the great Dublin brewery family,
only seventy years before; it was put back again in 1935. The hel-
mets and arms of the Knights of St Patrick still glower above their
stalls in the cathedral, but since the advent of the Irish Republic

the order has been decidedly attenuated; when in 1992 I asked the College of Heralds how many members it now had, I was told there were two – the Queen of England and the Knight Attendant of the Order (who wears, so the Duty Herald assured me when I observed that the knightly duties could not be very onerous, a most handsome badge of office).

Nevertheless when I visited St Patrick's one recent Sunday I found the cathedral full of former Royal Air Force men commemorating the Battle of Britain, medal ribbons gleaming and thumbs down the seams of their trousers.

It is very windy wet & cold, & I am sitting alone after lunch in the lounge with a grey black netting woman. The scene is St Stephen's Green [Dublin], an Irish attempt at Lincoln's Inn fields, just as Merrion Square attempts Bedford Sqre & so on. We lunched at the Sherburne [Shelburne Hotel]; & there are the film actors; here they are too. Aran islanders, in thick tweeds, who sit over the fire downstairs singing what may be hymns. I heard Irish for the first time . . . An air of inferiority sleeps or simpers or sneers or rages everywhere. A visitor from England brings back news of picture galleries, theatres. Here it is a mixture of Hampstead & Cambridge. At the Gate Theatre last night we were not sure which it was: there's an edge of difference, & the play was good: about Emmett, advanced, pseudo-Auden, I imagine. Three instruments to make music. A curtain that wdnt close; much satire of the Irish love of bloodshed; satire of the attempts at culture; a sudden sense came over me of being in the midst of history – that is of being in an unsettled, feverish place, which would have its period given it in the books; anything may happen. Yet what can happen when the best restaurant in the capital is Jammets, when there's only boiled potatoes in the biggest hotel in Dublin? Everywhere they seem to be living on watered wine. At last I gather why, if I were Irish, I should wish to belong to the Empire: no luxury, no creation, no stir, only the dregs of London, rather wish-washy as if suburbanised. Yet, I thought too at the Gate, they may have a spirit in them somewhere, that could make something, if freed. But they are freed, I continue – & indeed the play said, sardonically, & only this provinciality is the result . . .

No, it wouldnt do living in Ireland, in spite of the rocks & the desolate bays. It would lower the pulse of the heart: & all one's mind wd. run out in talk.

Diary, 6 May

The Aran islander actors were on their way home from England, where they had been taking part in the processing of Man of Aran, *Robert Flaherty's celebrated documentary film. The play at the Gate was* The Old Lady Says 'No'!, *by E. W. Tocher, which was about the eighteenth-century Irish revolutionary hero Robert Emmet. Jammets' Restaurant on Nassau Street, which Virginia Woolf seems to have scorned, was the scene of happy improvident evenings for James Joyce's family, and was generally much loved until it closed after the Second World War (during which its regular clientele included both Germans and Britons): I remember it in the austere years after the war as a very haven of* filet mignon. *Its premises are now Judge Roy Bean's Pub and Restaurant.*

Virginia, one notes, makes no reference to Joyce, whose Ulysses *had been declined by the Hogarth Press in 1918: her own* Mrs Dalloway, *which she began writing in 1922, and which she originally called* The Hours, *portrayed a single day in the life of London just as* Ulysses *portrayed a Dublin day.*

Germany

Virginia Woolf went three times to Germany, once shortly before the First World War, once in the time of the Weimar Republic, once during the Nazi regime. Pacifist that she was, she had decided early in life that she did not like Germanness. 'I can never quite get over the florid Teuton spirit, with its gross symbolism,' she wrote when she was in her twenties. 'You see in the common German type but a lump of crude earth, as yet unchiselled by the finger of time.' In the 1930s this conviction was doubtless reinforced by the fact that her husband was Jewish.

Bayreuth, 1909

In August 1909 Virginia went with her brother Adrian and a friend to the Wagner season at Bayreuth, Bavaria, then in its twenty-sixth year at the specially built Festspielhaus. Virginia bravely claimed to enjoy the operas, but she was not very musical, her German was vestigial, and one suspects she was not sorry when the visit ended.

We wandered about Bayreuth after we arrived. It is like an English market town – with a great many ironmongers, and a broad street with a fountain in the middle, and an

18th Century mayors house. Unfortunately the shops are full of cards and Holy Grails . . . We are very minute in our ways already. We sat and watched the people in the park for an hour. My God, they are hideous! The women have a strap round their waists, a green hunting cap, with a feather, and short skirts. They are never fashionable. I don't cause any horror. We dined at the foreigners restaurant, and even there they are incredibly stout and garish. Every young woman, too, brings an old housekeeper . . . to look after her. They eat enormously, off great joints, covered with fat.

Letter to Vanessa Bell, 7 August

We heard Parsifal yesterday – a very mysterious emotional work, unlike any of the others I thought. There is no love in it; it is more religious than anything. People dress in half mourning, and you are hissed if you try to clap. As the emotions are all abstract – I mean not between men and women – the effect is very much diffused; and peaceful on the whole. However, Saxon and Adrian say that it was not a good performance, and that I shant know anything about it until I have heard it 4 times. Between the acts, one goes and sits in a field, and watches a man hoeing turnips. The audience is very dowdy, and the look of the house is drab; one has hardly any room for ones knees, and it is very intense. I think earnest people only go – Germans for the most part, in sacks, with symbolical braid. Everything is new art – the restaurants have single lines drawn up the walls, with triangles suddenly bursting out – the kind of thing one sees in the Studio [the art magazine]. The grossness of the race is astonishing – but they seem very clean and kind.

Letter to Vanessa Bell, 8 August

. . . This afternoon, as it is an off day, we walked out to the Hermitage. This is a place built in imitation of Versailles;

and it is all overgrown and deserted, with little French Temples, and ruins, and courtyards. Wherever one goes, one finds a garden set with tables, where monster men and women drink great jugs of beer and eat meat – although it is a blazing hot day. The weather tends to break up. The colours are very beautiful – yellow and leaden. We walked home through the fields. I dont much admire the country, because it is very florid and without shadow; and one feels wedged into the earth, with no sea anywhere. However the town is charming; most of it built in the 18th century; there are very wide streets, with solid grey houses, like Cambridge houses, only somehow rather rustic. Last night we walked about after dinner, and all the people were singing over their beer. As there was very little light, and a few people peeping out of windows, and virgins tripping by in cloaks, and a great yellow coach standing in the middle of the road, one might have been in the year 1750.

Letter to Vanessa Bell, 10 August

It has been possible, during these last performances, to step out of the opera house and find oneself in the midst of a warm summer evening. From the hill above the theatre you look over a wide land, smooth and without hedges; it is not beautiful, but it is very large and tranquil. One may sit among rows of turnips and watch a gigantic old woman, with a blue cotton bonnet on her head and a figure like one of Dürer's, swinging her hoe. The sun draws out strong scents from the hay and the pine trees, and if one thinks at all, it is to combine the simple landscape with the landscape of the stage. When the music is silent the mind insensibly slackens and expands, among happy surroundings: heat and the yellow light, and the intermittent but not unmusical noises of insects and leaves smooth out the folds. In the next interval, between seven and eight, there is another act out here also: it is now dusky and perceptibly fresher; the light is thinner, and the roads are no longer crossed by regular bars of shade. The figures in light dresses moving

151

between the trees of the avenue, with depths of blue air behind them, have a curiously decorative effect. Finally, when the opera is over, it is quite late; and half way down the hill one looks back upon a dark torrent of carriages descending, their lamps wavering one above another, like irregular torches.

Article in **The Times,** *21 August*

Bayreuth is still in many ways rather like an English market town, down to the chain stores, the pedestrian areas, the evening louts and the Big Mac in Maximilianstrasse, and at a wedding I witnessed at the Hermitage one Saturday in 1992 the bride was chewing gum and had a wreath of flowers tipsily askew on her head. It is still possible to come out of the Festspielhaus (which was deliberately not built for comfort) and find oneself in remarkably rural surroundings; hundreds of people have carved their initials on the parapet outside the main entrance, during intervals I suppose, but I have not been able to find VW among them.

Five years later Virginia went to a performance of the Ring cycle in London, and determined that she would never go again – her eyes were bruised, her ears were dulled, her brain was pulped by its 'bawling sentimentality'.

Hitler's Reich, *1935*

'Never again,' Virginia wrote after her only visit to Berlin, in January 1929. She thought it 'the ugliest town in the world'. She had gone there with Leonard Woolf to visit Vita Sackville-West and her husband Harold Nicolson, who was serving in the British Embassy there. During their stay Virginia appears to have declared her love for Vita at the restaurant at the foot of the new Radio Tower ('The Beanpole'), one of the few monuments of the time that is still standing; she returned to England in a state of emotional and physical collapse. Six years later, nevertheless, she and Leonard spent three days in Germany during a motoring holiday around Europe, taking their marmoset Mitz with them. They felt greatly oppressed by the ideology of the Nazis, by then in

power, but all Virginia wrote about it were a few diary entries.

Sitting in the sun outside the German Customs. A car with the swastika on the back window has just passed through the barrier into Germany. L. is in the customs . . . Ought I go in & see what is happening? The Dutch Customs took 10 seconds. This has taken 10 minutes already. The windows are barred. Here they come out & the grim man laughed at Mitz. But L. said that when a peasant came in & stood with his hat on, the man said This office is like a Church & made him move it. Heil Hitler said the little thin boy opening his bag, perhaps with an apple in it, at the barrier. We become obsequious – delighted that is when the officers smile at Mitzi – the first stoop in our back . . .

Diary, 9 May

By the Rhine, sitting at the window . . . We were chased across the river by Hitler (or Goering) had to pass through ranks of children with red flags. They cheered Mitzi. I raised my hand. People gathering in the sunshine – rather forced like school sports. Banners stretched across the street 'The Jew is our enemy' 'There is no place for Jews in —'. So we whizzed along until we got out of range of the docile hysterical crowd. Our obsequiousness gradually turning to anger. Nerves rather frayed. A sense of stupid mass feeling masked by good temper.

Diary, 9 May

It was probably Goering who was being greeted by the crowds in Bonn, though it amused Virginia later to write that they had 'almost met Hitler face to face'.

We . . . drove down the Rhine. An ugly pretentious country – operatic scenery. High, but insignificant hills, bristling with black & green fir trees, with correct towers & ruins – a river that runs with coal barges like Oxford Street; traffic on

the cobbled roads . . . We got to Heidelberg, which is – yes –
a very distinguished university town on the Neckar. The
dons & their daughters were having a musical evening. I
saw them tripping out to each others houses with pale blue
Beethoven quartets under their arms . . . And next day to
Augsburg – a dull town . . . Augsburg to Innsbruck . . .
What did we see today? Great snow hills, with black rifts in
them. Torrents, Lakes; one copper green. And it rained for
the first time & was cold in the mountains. Fancy living
with dirty snow at the door in May! . . . The Hitler feeling
relaxed, though every village had a painted sign 'Die Juden
sind hier unwunscht'. But this seemed to be put up by
authority. Changed into Austria at last; & we are now
almost out of earshot.

*Virginia had left the two previous days of her diary blank, pre-
sumably in case Nazi officials should read it. 'L. says I may now
tell the truth, but I have forgotten 2 days of truth, & my pen is
weeping ink.'*

The Netherlands

1935

Virginia and Leonard spent a week motoring in the Netherlands in the summer of 1935.

... As for Holland: in the first place the cows wear coats; then the cyclists go in flocks like starlings, gathering together, skimming in & out. Driving is dangerous. Towns are large. They are also strung out, mile on mile. We are back in 1913. Everywhere there are shops full of clothes, food, books. The people are dressed in perfect respectability. Sailors wear felt hats. From 10 to 25 the girls are elegant, dove grey, slender, skimming on their cycles in & out. From 30 to 50 they amass vast bodies. But always the bodies are tight, spruce, shoes elegant hair beautifully done ... The houses are the glory of Holland – the richly carved big windowed houses; some lean a little, others are peaked; but each is a solid spruce perfectly self respecting house, in which last night I saw the Sunday diners, old men old women sitting round with children, cactuses; a cat & a dog. Amsterdam a swollen stone monster, shaved off like a ruin on the side of the marsh; our first lunch at the Hague had 20 courses ... Oh but the carved doors, the curved white facades, the lilac trees: the air of swept & garnished prosperity, antiquity, air, cleanliness . . .

Diary, 6 May

The plan of a Dutch town is: a bridge a canal: under an arch into a street: pointed stepped houses; orange and green awnings; 1620: on brand new garages: a great red brick tower, then a vast church, shut up . . . Flights of cyclists. Immense profusion of highly civilized shops – flower shops, shoes, bicycles, books, everything the more solidly placed wealthy but not frivolous citizen can eat or wear or use: all shining spick & span. English, French German books equal to Dutch. Shops upon shops. People pullulating. Not a beggar, not a slum . . . Angularity. A feeling that Holland is a perfectly self respecting rather hard featured but individual middle aged woman.

Diary, 8 May

I am . . . sitting in a teashop where 3 Dutch are have horns filled with cream. The nice girl smiles at me . . . The two children are eating cakes. Hoolarja, Dutchaboch! – it sounds like that. They dont have tea. A very spick & span shop. They laugh. I pretend to write postcards.

Diary, 8 May

France

France was the foreign country Virginia Woolf knew best – all educated English people knew France – but she wrote little about it. Not counting brief transit journeys, she went there sixteen times, spending in all about five months in the country. Her first visit was in 1896, when she was fourteen; her last was in 1939, with her husband Leonard, and this was her final excursion out of England. In her spasms of Francophilia she often thought of acquiring a house in France, but her inadequate French was a handicap, and she confined herself instead, in later years, to frequent motor tours.

Going to France
Essay in the Nation & Athenaeum, *5 May 1923*

You, who cross the Channel yearly, probably no longer see the house at Dieppe, no longer feel, as the train moves slowly down the street, one civilisation fall, another rise – from the ruin and chaos of British stucco this incredible pink and blue phœnix, four stories high, with its flower-pots, its balconies, its servant girl leaning on the window-sill, indolently looking out. Quite unmoved you sit reading – Thomas Hardy, perhaps – bridging abysses, preserving continuity, a little contemptuous of the excitement which is moving those who feel themselves liberated from one civilisation, launched upon another to such odd gestures, such strange irreticences. But reflect how much they have already gone through. Try to recall the look of London streets seen very early, perhaps very young, from a cab window on the way to Victoria. Everywhere there is the same intensity, as if the moment, instead of moving, lay suddenly still, became suddenly solemn, fixed the passers-by in their most transient aspects eternally. They do not know how important they have become. If they did, perhaps they would cease to buy newspapers and scrub door-steps. But we who are about to leave them feel all the more moved that they should continue to do these homely things on the brink of that precipice – our departure. Therefore it is natural that those who have survived the crossing, with its last scrutiny of passing faces so like a little rehearsal of death, should be shaken; should move hand-bags; start conversations; and tremble for one intoxicating moment upon the brink of that ideal society where every-one without fear or hesitation reveals the depths of his soul.

But it is only for a moment. Next, the disembodied spirit fluttering at the window desires above all things to be admitted to the new society where the houses are painted in lozenges of pale pink and blue; women wear shawls; trousers are baggy; there are crucifixes on hilltops; yellow mongrel dogs; chairs in the street; cobbles – gaiety, frivol-ity, drama, in short. 'I'm awfully sorry for Agnes, because now they can't be married till he gets a job in London. It's too far to get back from the works for midday dinner. I should have thought the father would have done some-thing for them.' These detached sentences, spoken a little brokenly (for they are frowning into tiny mirrors and drawing combs intently through fair bobbed hair) by two English girls, fall like the bars of a prison-house heavily across the mind. It is from them that we must escape; the hours, the works, the divisions, rigid and straight, of the old

British week. Already, as the train moved out of Dieppe, these obstructions seemed bubbling and boiling in the cauldron of a more congenial civilisation. The days of the week diminished; the hours disappeared. It was five o'clock, but no banks had simultaneously shut their doors, nor from innumerable lifts had millions of citizens emerged in time for dinner, or in the poorer suburbs for slices of cold meat and Swiss roll laid orderly in shallow glass dishes. There must be divisions, even for the French, but where they fall we cannot tell, and the lady in the corner, so pale, so plump, so compact, seemed as she sat smiling to be riding life over ditches and boundaries smoothed out by the genius of the Latin race.

She rose to go to the dining car. As she sat down she took a small frying-pan from her handbag and hid it discreetly beneath a tent made from a copy of *Le Temps*. Deftly, as each dish was served, she secreted a portion in the absence of the waiter. Her husband smiled. Her husband approved. We only knew that she was brave. They might be poor. The helpings were large. The French have mothers. To redress perpetually the extravagances of life, and make the covering fit the fact instead of bulging in ostentatious emptiness, was part, no doubt, of the French genius for living. Still, when it comes to the thick, yellow rind of a not fresh cheese – Ironically smiling, she condescended, in that exquisite tongue which twinkles like diamonds with all its accents, to explain that she kept a dog. But she might have kept – anything. 'Life is so simple,' she seemed to say.

'Life is so simple – life is so simple,' said the wheels of the Sud Express all night long in that idiotic or ironic way they have, for any message less appropriate to the uneasy darkness, the clank of chains, the anguished cries of railwaymen, and, in the dawn, the misery of the unrested body could scarcely be imagined. But travellers are much at the mercy of phrases. Taken from home, which, like a shell, has made them hard, separate, individual, vast generalisations formulate in their exposed brains; the stress of

wheel or window-blind beats into rhythm idiotic sayings of
false profundity about life, repeats to distraction fragments
of prose, and makes them stare with ferocious melancholy
at the landscape, which, in the middle of France, is dull
enough. The French are methodical; but life is simple; the
French are prosaic; the French have roads. Yes, they have
roads which strike from that lean poplar there to Vienna, to
Moscow; pass Tolstoy's house, climb mountains, then
march, all shop decorated, down the middle of famous
cities. But in England the road runs out on to a cliff; wavers
into sand at the edge of the sea. It begins to seem dangerous
to live in England. Here actually one could build a house
and have no neighbours; go for a walk along this eternal
white road for two, three, four miles, and meet only one
black dog and one old woman who, depressed perhaps by
the immensity of the landscape and the futility of loco-
motion, has sat herself down on a bank, attached her cow
to her by a rope, and there sits, unmoved, incurious, monu-
mental. Could our English poets for a moment share her
seat and think her thoughts, forget the parish, the pansy,
and the sparrow's egg, and concentrate (as she appears to
do) upon the fate of man!

In the South

*In 1925 Virginia and Leonard spent twelve days at the fishing
village of Cassis, near Marseilles, which was popular with the
English in those days.*

I am waiting to see what form of itself Cassis will finally cast
up in my mind. There are the rocks. We used to go out after
breakfast & sit on the rocks, with the sun on us. L. used to
sit without a hat, writing on his knee. One morning he
found a sea urchin — they are red, with spikes which quiver
slightly. Then we would go a walk in the afternoon, right
up over the hill, into the woods, where one day we heard
the motor cars & discovered the road to La Ciota[t] just

beneath. It was stony, steep & very hot. We heard a great chattering birdlike noise once, & I bethought me of the frogs. The ragged red tulips were out in the fields; all the fields were little angular shelves cut out of the hill, & ruled & ribbed with vines; & all red, & rosy & purple here & there with the spray of some fruit tree in bud. Here & there was an angular white, or yellow or blue washed house, with all its shutters tightly closed; & flat paths round it, & once rows of stocks; an incomparable cleanness & definiteness every-where. At La Ciota[t] great orange ships rose up out of the blue water of the little bay. All these bays are very circular, & fringed with the pale coloured plaster houses, very tall, shuttered, patched & peeled, now with a pot & tufts of green on them, now with clothes, drying; now an old old woman looking. On the hill, which is stony as a desert, the nets were drying; & then in the streets children & girls gos-siped & meandered all in pale bright shawls & cotton frocks, while the men picked up the earth of the main square to make a paved court of it.

Diary, 8 April 1925

Two years later Virginia's sister Vanessa, with her husband Clive Bell and her lover Duncan Grant, established themselves in a house at Cassis, and three times the Woolfs went to visit them there, at one time taking serious steps to acquire a house for them-selves nearby. Virginia was much attracted by the free-and-easy atmosphere of the arrangements.

Then Colonel Teed and Miss Campbell come to lunch – he a retired cavalry officer, she his mistress: both together vine growers, living in a divine 17th Century manor house, set with cypresses, painted, tiled, with tanks of frogs and Roman aqueducts. Miss Campbell was sitting in the dusk listening to the frogs last night when we went there. So there we all sat quite silent; and then the frogs began again; and the Colonel made us come in and drink several dif-ferent kinds of wine in his great empty room, and we were given bunches of wild tulips, Vita, and why don't we all live like that, Vita? – and never go back to Bloomsbury any more? You meet a Miss Brown here, and she says her eldest son is 17. Yes. She has three children by the Italian singing master in Genoa. Madame Labrotte was afflicted with a gigantic tumour – had all the doctors of London and Paris to consult – came to Cassis to recuperate and was delivered, at the age of 50, in one quarter of an hour, of a child. That is our atmosphere – slightly detached, from reality . . . mute: they are all painters: every street corner has an elderly gentleman on a camp stool; austere; The sink of the bath has to be filled with flannel: Clive does it for me: I stand in a chemise with jugs of cold water, since the pipe is blocked. Our grand extravagance is wine, which the peasants sell, and Clive and Duncan fetch in great baskets, dressed in cotton clothes, with rope slippers: Duncan smuggles brandy in, and so we sit, talking, for hours . . .

Letter to Vita Sackville-West, 5 April 1927

Colonel Teed was a retired Indian Army officer, Miss Campbell a former Army nurse. On later visits Virginia and Leonard stayed at their property, Château Fontcreuse, on the hill behind the town, where the Colonel lived in an ebulliently eccentric style. Fontcreuse still makes excellent red and white wines, and down a track among the vineyards one may visit La Bergère, the little house, in a sad state in 1992, where the Woolfs stayed.

It was the image of a night-moth at Cassis that inspired Virginia Woolf's book The Waves *(originally called* The Moths*). Later, under the influence of Tuscany, she turned against the landscapes of southern France, and wrote of their 'black & green violent monotonous hills'.*

A Holiday Tour, *1931*

In the spring of 1931 Virginia and Leonard enjoyed one of their happiest French holidays, driving from Dieppe to the Bordeaux region, and back by a hedonistically roundabout route.

Very wet: very cold: horrid seaside marine atmosphere: all drenched & shrubs blown as usual at Dieppe. Breakfast in the usual hotel [du Rhinet de Newhaven]. Started. Wind & rain: almost black air. Rain came through. At the ferry at Quilleboeuf L. saw blue sky. Great rejoicing. Lunch at Inn by ferry – cheap, coarse; burnt fish. Old man & woman country people lunching. He had a thimble of brandy in his coffee.

Diary, 17 April

Went to Fontevrault. Saw beautiful bare old convent church. Dont take off your hat, said man. Its not sacred. The tombs of Plantagenets: like Edith Sitwell: straight, narrow side by side: re-painted, blue & red. Now all this great convent where filles de France educated a prison. Prison bells ringing for their dinner. Fountain where the girls washed before dinner. The cold must have been worse then. The Abbesses had themselves painted in frescoes – fat, sensual, highnosed faces.

Diary, 18 April

Fontevrault (or Fontevraud), the great monastery near Saumur which was the necropolis of the Plantagenets, had been a prison since 1804, and was to remain one until 1963: one of its best-known inmates was to be the writer Jean Genet, who thought it the most disturbing prison he knew. It is now a cultural centre, with a hotel, and when I was there in 1992 a man inspecting the tombs of the Plantagenets (who certainly do look remarkably Sitwellian) was in fact wearing a cloth cap.

Virginia's visit to the castle at Chinon, where Joan of Arc first met King Charles VII of France (then still called the Dauphin, or heir to the throne), was perhaps partly inspired by the fact that her friend Vita Sackville-West was particularly interested in Joan, and would presently (1936) publish a biography of her.

Explored castle alone ... Saw the high unroofed room in wh. Jeanne stood before the King. The very chimney piece perhaps. Walls cut through by thin windows. Suddenly one looks down, down on roofs. How did the middle ages get through the evenings? A stone crypt in wh. J. lived: people carve their names everywhere. River silken serpentine beneath. Liked the stone roofless rooms; & the angular cut windows. Sat on the steps to hear 2 struck by the clock wh. has rung since the 13th Century: wh. J. heard. Rusty tone. What did she think? Was she mad? a visionary coinciding with the right moment.

Diary, 27 April

All at Chinon is still as it was then, and the clock is striking rustily still.

I voted for Dreux; so we went there – to Hotel de Paradis; & coming in heard the violins, & saw thinly dressed girls; cheap; rigged out in ready mades from the local shop. A wedding. Dancing already at 5.30. This is the Inn that has old cupboards. Had to dine across the yard, as the dining room was danced in. Strawberries for dinner ... All very slow & cold. People driving up in cars all the time. Little boys scampering about in black velvet. Small girl perfectly dressed & very prim. Whole families invited: small business people I imagine. The dancing went on till 11. Then we saw the wretched waiters carrying tables across – how cynical all waiters must be & chambermaids – how terribly aware of the transitoriness of life – & the music stopped. They ate. Then at 12 or 1 (I was woken) cars began tuning up: people shouting, laughing saying goodbye. I had seen the bride dancing – a pale girl in spectacles – & thought of her borne off to fulfil her duties in some small suburban house outside Dreux, for she was marrying a clerk I should think: & they now begin to replenish the race.

Diary, 27 April

Walk yesterday [from Brantôme]. Forgot the size of maps. Found Champagnac beyond us. Went wrong at Les Roches. Arrived at an old house on a green sward, with trees & walled garden. O to live here, we said. So much subtler, gentler, lovelier than Cassis. The land is flat & green as a lawn; with elongated quivering poplars just fledged; then the spade pressed hills I love; & the river, by which we walked – the river so deep, so romantic, taking the blue thunder clouds, the willows, twisting them nonchalantly, flowing on. Clumps of purple gentian in the reeds. An Elizabethan meadow – cowslips, bluebells. But the thunder roared out. We ran. We sheltered under a ruined cave of some sort. Then dashed home 2 miles of road or more; thighs aching; thunder & lightning at Cemetery. All the tin shelters & metal wreaths gleamed. Girls, mourners, took arms & ran. Home before the main shower, very heavy.

Diary, 25 April

Actually the country around Brantôme is rolling and thickly wooded, but it still contains many desirable old houses, much in demand among the English expatriates Virginia preferred to keep clear of.

Went to Marennes, across an emerald green marsh: deserted, a cow or two: a tall spare woman dressed in black like a clergyman. At Bourgeant? [Brouage] – a town in an old wall; tufted with grass. Lovely country. a ferry. aeroplanes looping loop. Church in Marennes; old ship slung from ceiling. The hotel of the oysters 2 Ki. on. Sat at green table in the sun & drank coffee: L. had 12 oysters: alive: twisted in his mouth he said; green: with distorted shells. A pine wood; all silent; no bungalows. low sea. boats out at oyster banks. Very lovely drive back across the marsh. Tall marsh grasses fine yellow like babies' hair: broad brown river.

Diary, 21 April

Marenne, south of La Rochelle, is the capital of the green oyster, and its restaurants still loudly advertise Degustation Huîtres. *In the church the suspended model of the three-masted warship* Saint Pierre, *bristling with guns, rotates slightly with the breeze through the open door.*

The destination that meant most to Virginia, on this cheerful tour, was the château at St Michel de Montaigne, near Bordeaux, where her literary hero Michel de Montaigne wrote his essays.

Rang at Castle door. No one came. Women tending cows in ancient stables. A tower at one end. A garden with flowering trees. The usual renovated peaked & black tiled Chateau: over the door Que S'cais-je – A woman came. Took us up narrow stone steps, worn; opened thick nail studded door. This is his bedroom; this is his dressing room. Here he died. Here he went down – he was very small – to Chapel. Upstairs again is his library. The books & furniture are at Bordeaux. Here is his chair & table. He wrote those inscriptions on the beams. Sure enough it was his room; a piece of an old wooden chair might be his. A circular tower, very thick; 3 small windows looking along the wall to another tower. All that remains of the fire wh. burnt the old Chateau in 1880 – or thereabouts. We wandered on the terrace. Saw the vineyards below; the shaped reddish hills & terraces: one or two brooding brown farms – much his view – the curious musing man must have halted to look at what we saw. So lovely now; as then. Americans &c. Every day of the year the woman said. A dog went with us fetching a chestnut & putting it on the parapet to be thrown.

Diary, 25 April

My word Ethel, the very door he opened is there: the steps, worn into deep waves, up to the tower: the 3 windows: writing table, chair, view, vine, dogs, everything precisely as it was – when? – I cant remember. Also 4 ancient saddles.

Letter to Ethel Smyth, 24 April

At the end, where I have, with trembling fingers after a whole bottle of Monbazillac, drawn an arrow, Montaigne wrote his essays. There we went this morning: a divine country all round – vineyards, oxen, spring. We must come again together. O so drunk; and have eaten a whole paté de foie gras.

Postcard to Vita Sackville-West, 23 April

When I went to Montaigne's tower in 1992 a bouncing jolly dog, perhaps a descendant of Virginia's guide, welcomed me to the château before gambolling off with a mongrel friend through the sunlit deserted village. I was trespassing – the château is closed to the public on Mondays and its gates were closed: it was the dog that had persuaded me to climb over the fence.

Monte Carlo
Diary, 28 May 1935

A bright blue & white day: carved parapets gleaming; little embayed town on the sea. I saw domes & pillars & told L. this was the Casino; so we went in, & had to produce passports, & sign a paper, & give up hat & umbrella, & then paid nothing but went into a florid but dingy hall, set with seven or eight tables, something like great billiard tables, at which sat a dingy sweaty rather sordid crew, with their faces all set & expressionless watching the gold bars sweeping this way & that in the middle. They had something peculiar. One couldnt place them. Some were dingy old governesses in spectacles, others professors with beards; there was one flashy adventuress; but most were small business men – only rather, not very vicious. It was a blazing hot Sunday morning about 12, & this, we thought is the way our culture spends its holidays. Vicious, dull, & outside lurid. So on.

In Chartres

Diary, 29 May 1935

And, putting down my pen, I fetched L. & we went to the
Cathedral which was almost dark & melodramatic – I mean
surprising, there only the arches & shadows showing, we
all alone, & the blue windows blazing in the cold grey
night. In fact it was like seeing the skeleton & eyes of the
cathedral glowing there. Mere bones, & the blue red eyes.
The windows are all blue & red, & at one end there's the
jewel burning – the great rose jewel, burning blue in coal
blackness, for all the world like something worn upon a
vast – what? woman['s] body wont do. The jewel of the
world then – or is that sentimental? After we had sat &
looked slowly grayness returned to the thick pillars but still
the scooped (shadowy) look remained. Never had we seen
it so bare, so architectural, a statement of proportions, save
for the fiery & deep blue glass, for the glass varied from
gloomy to transcendent. So back to a first rate dinner – a
dinner thought out, & presided over by a graceful young
chef, precisely like Raymond [Mortimer?], only with
greater gift & charm. For instance he concocted a sauce out
of cream, French beans, mustard, salt & wine. To add the
wine he held his finger which was not clean half over the
mouth of the bottle. Then left the sauce to simmer over a
spirit lamp: then another red brown casserole was brought,
& the sauce poured over. Our dinner was rich & thought-
ful: I had mushrooms in cream. And I observed the way a
good waiter serves a dish with infinite care & respect, as if
handling something precious. Now Chartres is quieter, & so
to sleep.

French Places
Albi, Tarn

A flashy hotel; circle of blue and red electric light in the hall which went in and out. Bad dinner. The worst hotel yet found. Walked in the rain. Cathedral magnificent – like factory in red: firm, fluted, rock-like, painted within . . . Rain all night. Room thick with dust. Walls stained – bugs possibly.

Journal, May 1937

Alençon, Orne

A white elegant old town, with a great magnolia tree all stuck thick with flowers. Heard a loudspeaker in an old house, where a girl sat under rows of jars writing . . . Vast bare Place for soldiers.

Diary, 17 April 1931

Angoulême, Charente

Slightly reminded me of Clifton [Bristol, England] – high airy terraces, overlooking breadths of cloud darkened country. Girls drinking port & eating cakes in Thé Salon.

Diary, 25 April 1931

Avallon, Yonne

A very charming old place . . . sublime view; and tower, churches, old houses, patisseries and antiquaries *ad lib* . . . The donkey population is large and in the highest degree monotonous.

Letter to Leonard Woolf, 27 September 1928

Brantôme, Dordogne

A fine evening, a stone bridge, a river going in circles like the lash of a whip; a boy fishing, a man cutting down a poplar tree: And a whole colony of gypsies nested in a rock.

Letter to Vita Sackville-West, 24 April 1931

Carnac, Morbihan (the megalithic monuments)

Somehow impressive, like an army of old washerwomen emerging from primeval times, each with a sheet on her head.

Letter to Ethel Smyth, 18 June 1939

Elsewhere Virginia Woolf called the megaliths 'tombs'.

La Rochelle, Charente-Maritime

It looks like Bologna [Italy], – arches I mean: roofs made of red flower pots; a lilac in full flower; roman remains in the garden below the window. A very nice hotel, the floor shining; a toothless old servant in black; a hint of imagination in the sauces: the south beginning to warm and tumble.

Letter to Ethel Smyth, 20 April 1931

The hotel was the France-Angleterre, now in a different location, but still with shiny floors.

Le Mans, Sarthe

Grey & white curved, dignified, flat windowed ancient town.

Diary, 27 April 1931

Plus the annual 24-hour motor race, which had been run since 1923.

Maintenon, Eure-et-Loir

Old claws of ruin against the bright evening sky after dinner. Birds singing; many nightingales, very fine and pure. All silent and unspoilt.

Journal, May 1937

Meyronne, Lot

Great day at Meyronne, where I wish to live – up to the castle. An old woman shredding salsify. Talked about wild boars – sometimes killed; quite tame; they eat them . . . The farm with the great pigeon house; all these old things not preserved but used and allowed to fall into decay.

Journal, May 1937

Virginia could at least take rooms in the castle now, for it has been turned into a hotel.

Najac, Aveyron

Sordidly medieval; bossed, with great beams; and muffled grinning heads; round a mediaeval fountain. No place for human beings to live in – the middle ages. Houses perched on top of cliff. River flattened out beneath. An unreal dead crawling quiet, as if they were inhabiting an old shell. The old men gossipping with their pointed walking sticks. No life; no shops; dirt and misery.

Journal, May 1937

Najac is now an all too well promoted tourist destination, generally considered one of the most picturesque villages in France.

Périgueux, Dordogne

Old furniture shops: expensive chairs: a church with green domes; scraped; renewed. All worshippers are old women; all in black; all woollen; decrepit. A random priest ambling along with different gestures.

Diary, 25 April 1931

The 'church with green domes' is the vast and astonishing Byzantine cathedral of Saint-Front – five domes, a dozen minarets and a spired bell-tower.

Rodez, Aveyron

The best hotel in the world. Spirits sprung up. A long walk after tea. Sat and looked at the mountains over the very green flat nightingale valley ... a very fine rust red cathedral.

Journal, May 1937

Souillac, Lot

There it became two hundred years ago. There we sat on the banks of the Dordogne in the evening and saw the man in the great hat and gaiters, and women washing clothes on the shingle. There was a cabin built against the rock like a scene in a play; and a man sitting there while the women went in and out. All this I said happened two hundred years ago ... Roofs here like high felt hats pulled down with a dent in the middle.

Journal, May 1937

Souillac is now well into the twentieth century, and those roofs are a mystery: I could find nothing remotely hat-like in the skyline of 1992.

Treignac, Haute-Vienne

Went walking to the top of the mountain to find the druid stones; all drenched green under trees; cuckoo calling; a little shepherds farm; rain coming down in full flood; as we went up following arrows, paths twisting; divine views all misted and shrouded; green lit ... Should be seen again, so lovely was it even then.

Journal, May 1937

Uzerche, Corrèze

We saw a woman sewing a white cloth on the banks of the river. She called the cows which obeyed ... The flowers were like an Elizabethan meadow. A man chopped wood in the wood above., I could hear the hollow sounds. No other sound. And a boy showed us the way, opening the door of a great barn ... A man at the garage ... said how he'd been in Gambia, and longed to be there not in this dead alive French village; where his wifes parents made him live.

Journal, May 1937

Vannes, Morbihan

A most sympathetic dignified town, with a quay, blue ships, old walls, old women marching about in black velvet robes with white caps, and in short all that one needs.

Letter to Vanessa Bell, 13 June 1939

Italy

Italy, where 'I shall come to die', Italy with the loveliest women in Europe, Italy 'the most beautiful of all lands anywhere' – Virginia Woolf's responses to Italy were, especially in later life, hyperbolic. Between 1904 and 1935 she went there seven times, not counting passage through the country by train from Greece and Turkey.

An Italian Journey
Journal, September 1908

There is not much to be said of Milan; unless it be that we entered here into Italian life. We walked out in the busy noisy streets, & felt irresponsible; tramped in the roadway; looked about a great deal without thinking much – understood vaguely that the populace were of the same mood.

There are great flat houses painted some clear colour, & decorated with bright green squares, at intervals. Flower pots make a graceful festoon of leaves on some of the ledges. It is all a little dusty, very dramatic – yellow walls defined against green plumage of parks. You exclaim Oh – & Ah – at the corners – so different from an English town in the provinces. I liken it to a sketch in water colour, by some spirited though not quite excellent master hand. It is much more sincere & sure of itself than we are, in our Brightons & Oxfords, as though done after some design, which the nature of colour & climate suggested.

We visited the Cathedral [of Siena], on the occasion of some festival. It is striped black & white, with rose colour & blue in the arches; golden knobs; a ceiling of azure; fruits, faces, beasts, carved on every pinnacle or angle. In the chapels there were glittering images, & candles; & the high altar had all its tiers of wax alight. There were gorgeous priests, ministering here, with their backs to us, from which yellow satins gold embroidered, hung in stiff squares. One had a white hat, like the petal of a cyclamen, on his head.

It was the feast of the Virgin, & a large crowd, in their Sunday dress, had come to worship. A strange worship compared with ours! Instead of rank of seats, movements all in order, & a service like a military performance, no single worshipper here knew what his neighbour did or seemed to attend to the clerical commands. The priests themselves were passing & repassing, forming into lines, changing vestments, & rapidly carrying on the ceremonials all the time, as though they were doing a mystic rite, not understood by the people. The people looked, wandered about, sank on their knees, & rose again; their faith seemed warm & private, not to be regulated by any common need. I fancied, however, that this very decorative performance did represent to them the sacred body of their religion; sealed within these yellow & inlaid casks – I supposed that all the glories of the Heavens had this tangible form for them – the more impressive because of all these mysterious weavings & symbols.

They smell the flowers that grew in the holy fields; imagine the Cross risen, & the body upon it; it is all yellow stained, splendid, & remote. Are these priests – or are they not rather people who were present at the scene themselves? The Bishop sat on his carved throne, with his buckled shoes pompously displayed, his hands hid beneath his satin apron, & his face composed into a mask of rosy wax, smooth, & not a little contemptuous of earthly strife.

When you walk out of the front door here [Perugia] you find yourself apparently upon a parade, with the sea beneath. A blue vapour fills in the spaces between the white columns of the parapet; & the people are leaning & looking over, as they do at the sea side. But in truth it is dry land beneath, dropped down some distance; there are curved vineyards, groves of olives, & the hills which rise against the sky seem about on the level of our heads. At sunset, of course, there is a tremendous display; clouds of flamingo scarlet, & of the shape of curled feathers; spaces of crimson, with bars upon them; hills laid against the furnace so that their little fringe of trees is visible; but I like the fore-ground best with its soft green & brown, & its highest light the dull white enamel of the road.

After tea, instead of rummaging the streets after the fashion of our compatriots, we choose one of the roads which we can follow from our windows, & descend into the valley. Small paths branch at intervals, & lead between the vineyards. They are stony; lead past little square farms, washed salmon pink. Italian peasants are driving their ploughs through earth which has the appearance of extreme antiquity; it is so brown & dry that all the oil which holds the clods together must have been baked out of it. A pair of oxen, who are unwieldy & much given to contemplation, carry out this clumsy labour, & are of great value, for the sake of their creamy white colour, in the brown & grey landscape.

It is perhaps because I compare Umbrian vineyards with English fields that I am slow to come at any picture of this place. The divisions at first seemed to me perplexing: I found no solitude & no wildness; there were no deep clumps of shade, no fields with long grasses. The ground is singularly bare, & stony; brittle looking granaries of old pink brick, are dotted here & there, & perhaps there is an archway where women sit, handling maize. The snug circle of our farmyard does not exist. But the place is beautiful; the twisted little trees, now green, now black against the sky, are full of lines; lovely are the peaks in the distance, like a great encampment of tents of all sizes; here before us is Perugia on its hill, with all its long towers & square blocks massed in out line; there is no softness, nothing indistinct, but I begin to see that there is a character in this land, with its gnarled little trees, & its sharp outlines, which would soon make all other scenery insipid.

We spent the day at Assisi. It fronts us, on its hill top, some sixteen miles away, & between lies a perfectly flat space, lined with rows of trees, bearing the Tiber upon it. Assisi is another of these pyramid-shaped towns, which ascend with tier upon tier of whitish brown houses, till they culminate in a dome, or a long gallery of arches. Immense bare hills lie behind the town. When we had inspected the church we strolled through the streets. As usual, the houses are very high, & the streets narrow, so that if you laid a strip of roof across the top you would make a deep tunnel. In this instance the houses were rather splendid, with great windows & balconies, door ways fortified with stone, but all the shutters were up, or swung open idly, so that you could fancy great empty rooms within. The streets were deserted, save for a donkey cart, or an old woman squatted against the wall. The hills & the wide stretch of country visible beneath you at the end of every street seem to make these cities a little incongruous. They seem to cling peacefully to their hill top – to offer lodgment for besieged men & women, who no longer require it.

By 'the church' I take it Virginia means the double church in the Convent of St Francis, with its twenty-eight marvellous frescos by Giotto and his pupils – not often so summarily dismissed.

We are very leisurely travellers. We dip into one church or gallery in the morning, sit in our shaded rooms till it is time for tea, & the whole of our exercise consists of a gentle walk in the sunset . . . There are hills encircling us [in Umbria], which soon grow blue, though they rarely carry much weight of clouds upon them. The trees on our eminence glow, as though some yellow painters-medium were brushed over them. It is infinitely pleasant to sit & let the heat of the day recede, till a breeze springs, & it is time for dinner. There are flowers with voluminous yellow petals, in the gardens, & trees decorated as with red rosettes. They have few leaves to bear such splendour.

. . . The earth affords no shelter, no soft places, but every foots space of it is laid bare to the eye. There are single roads, one suspects, leading from village to village. On every eminence a large white or brown villa has perched itself, so that the land, though so wild, is not lonely. No park, or clump of trees hide these naked places . . . You get the impression of an immensely old civilization; for the land everywhere is under the eyes of the cultivator, & no stretch of it is left alone.

Anglo-Italians

Although Virginia Woolf often thought of acquiring a home abroad, she had a keen cool eye for the characteristics of English expatriates, who abounded in Italy in the early years of the century.

One old lady, in particular, seems to have been sitting there [in the Brufani Palace Hotel, Perugia] since the early fifties of the last century. She has spent her life, so far as she will reveal it, in travelling & testing the merits of different pensions. She pronounces the table here the best in Italy. At the same time she shows no enthusiasm; the life of a lodger is one of perpetual hostility.

Poor, a spinster, who begins to grow old, to travel is

really her most agreeable life. I figure her the Aunt of large families of little country gentry; she has a certain distinction because she can talk of her travels. She professes to find English life lacking in colour, & sets off on these long rambling peregrinations, from one cheap pension to another, never leaving the hackneyed towns, or seeing much in them. She sits all day in a corner of the dining room, knitting, or writing in a fretful hand long letters to old friends; she waits for meals & watches the dish on its way round the table. Certain old gentilities forbid her to gobble openly, & in the pauses between the plates she discharges a vast amount of faded learning, savouring of the 60s, when she drove over the Apennines in a great sun bonnet. She knows nothing accurately, but arrogates to herself a certain authority because she first saw pictures fifty years ago . . .

Now & then, excited by an eddy of life, she ventures out into the full current of general talk – & volunteers some correction or theory of her own – at which we can only be silent, or perhaps, trusting her infirmities, smile in secret; she flounders deep, suspects some hostility, flushes, becomes emphatic – & tries to overawe us with a tremulous flourish, or venerable authorities. Poor old Lady! This venture was unsuccessful, & she retires to mumble peevishly, but her brain sinks into torpor once more. Food consoles her.

Journal, September 1908

The worst of distinguished old ladies, who have known everyone and lived an independent life, is that they become brusque and imperious without sufficient wits to alleviate the manner. Mrs Ross lives in a great villa, is the daughter of distinguished parents; the friend of writers, and the character of the country side. She sells things off her walls. She is emphatic, forcible, fixes you with her straight grey eye as though it were an honour to occupy, even for a moment, its attention. The head is massive, it is held high; the mouth is coarse and the upper lip haired. Such old women like men, and have a number of unreasonable traditions. Pride of birth, I thought I detected; certainly she has that other pride, the pride which comes to those who have lived among the chosen spirits of the time. A word of family, and her wits were at work at once.

I know not why, but this type ... does not much attract me. Only one position is possible if you are a young woman: you must let them adopt queenly airs, with a touch of the maternal. She summons you to sit beside her, lays her hand for a moment on yours, dismisses you the next, to make room for some weakly young man. She has them to stay with her for months – likes them best when they are big and strong but will tolerate weakness for the sake of the sex. She has led a bold life, managing for herself, and an Englishwoman who dictates to peasants is apt to become domineering. However, there can be no question of her spirit – many portraits showed the intent indomitable face, in youth and middle age, it is still the same, beneath white hair. It proved her power that her drawing room filled with guests. She seemed to enjoy sweeping them about, without much ceremony. Parties were bidden to admire the garden; young men were commanded to hand cake.

Diary, 25 April 1909

Janet Ross (1842–1927), who lived at Settignano, outside Florence, was the daughter of the formidably unconventional writer and adventurer Lucie Duff-Gordon: but she had not 'by any means' (says Lady Duff-Gordon's biographer, Gordon Waterfield), 'as wide a range of interests and sympathy' as her mother.

In Syracuse
Letter to Vanessa Bell, 14 April 1927

We got here last night, and who should we meet driving from the station, but Osbert Sitwell, who stopped the cab and was very friendly, but he is lodged in a grand hotel outside the town, whereas we lodge in a cheap Italian inn, where no one speaks English, and we get delicious food, and there are only Italian officers and widows, and thank God, no Germans – so I dont suppose we shall see Osbert. There is a courtyard, with two cats in a basket, a waiter varnishing a table and an old woman picking over mattresses: I am rapidly falling in love with Italy. I think it is much more congenial than France – All the men must be womanisers. The old innkeeper cooks an omelette specially for me . . .

Last night we explored Syracuse by moonlight. But how am I to describe without boring you, particularly as you won't have drunk a bottle of wine, and be half tipsy as I was – the bay, the schooners, the blue sky, with the white pillars, like paper, and clouds crossing, and people sauntering, and a man on stilts – no it cant be done . . . I should like to go on travelling from town to town all my life, rambling about ruins and watching schooners come in, and falling in love with Italian girls.

Venice

Virginia Woolf went three times to Venice, in 1904 with a family party of five, in 1912 on her honeymoon, and in 1932 with her husband, their friend Roger Fry and his sister Margery.

There never was such an amusing and beautiful place. We have a room here right at the top just at the side of the Grand Canal: beneath all the gondolas are moored, and the gondoliers make such a noise I cant think coherently. It was the strangest dream to step out into our gondola after those two days of train . . . I can't believe it is a real place yet and I wander about open-mouthed . . . We walked all down the [Riva degli] Schiavoni last night – where the buildings looked cut out of marble, and a great gondola hung with coloured lamps floated by. But I cant find words yet . . .

Letter to Violet Dickinson, 4 April 1904

Their rooms were at the Grand Hotel on the Grand Canal. It occupied the Palazzo Fini, now government offices but next door to the Gritti Palace. Virginia called it 'a horrible big hotel', and after ten days her Venetian euphoria had worn off – she felt 'like a Bird in a Cage'. But as she said, five was too many for a visit to Venice, just as one was too few: she never forgot seeing, during her honeymoon there, a friend forlornly all alone in the Piazza.

One picture I saw – Phil Burne Jones [Sir Philip Burne-Jones] sitting in the square of St Mark's, in evening dress, alone one August night in 1912 . . . He looked dissipated & lonely, like a pierrot who had grown old & rather peevish. He wore a light overcoat & sat, his foolish nervous white face looking aged & set unhappy & eager & disillusioned, alone at a little marble table, while everyone else paraded or chattered & the band played – he had no companion – none of his smart ladies – nobody to chatter to, in his affected exaggerated voice . . .

Diary, 22 August 1929

On her third visit, en route *to Greece, Virginia 'only had time for 3 churches and part of the Academia' – a night and half a day.*

We take a gondola for one hour, & so cross to San Giorgio; & see the miraculous apse, & peer; & climb; & smooth our soles on the red yellow rosy pavement, raying out like the sea, with inlaid flowers: & Venetian light is pale & bright . . . Out after the play, in the theatre slung with green glass beads, onto the black tossing water, so silent, so swaying: & the poor people asked us not to overpay the traghetto [public ferry]; & there were cactuses; & a man singing in the morning; and R. [Roger] & I went to the Tiepolo church [probably the Gesuati]; & the thick yellow service with the priests weaving a web in incantation, & the little boys & the reverence & secularity & ancientness made us say This is the magic we want: & magic there must be; so long as magic keeps its place.

Diary, 18 April 1932

To Tuscany, *1933*

In the early summer of 1933 Virginia and Leonard Woolf drove through France and down the Italian Riviera to Tuscany, half-thinking as they travelled that they might settle somewhere along the route.

. . . We don't like the French Riviera, or the Italian much; but if it has to be, Rapallo does it best: its bay stretched with gold silk this evening, humming scented villas; all orange blossom. Quiet women reading to children, little boats, high cliffs; a sauntering indolent luxurious evening place, where one might spend ones last penny; grown old . . .

But we dont wish to live here, shredding out our days, in these scented villas, sauntering around the harbour.

Diary, 11 May

Max Beerbohm, who in later years did not much care for Virginia's diaries, had been living and sauntering in Rapallo since 1910. In the summer of 1992 the town seemed to me a perfect nightmare of congestion, as the holiday traffic crawled and sweltered by nose to tail for Portofino.

Yes Shelley chose better than Max Beerbohm. He chose a harbour [at Lerici]; a bay; & his home, with a balcony, on which Mary stood, looks out across the sea. Sloping sailed boats were coming in this morning – a windy little town, of high pink & yellow Southern houses, not much changed I suppose; very full of the breaking of waves, very much open to the sea; & the rather desolate house standing with the sea just in front. Shelley, I suppose, bathed, walked sat on the beach there; and Mary & Mrs Williams had their coffee on the balcony. I daresay the clothes & the people were much the same. At any rate, a very good great man's house in its way . . .

Shelley's house waiting by the sea, & Shelley not coming, & Mary & Mrs Williams watching from the balcony &

then Trelawney coming from Pisa & burning the body on the shore – thats in my mind.

Diary, 12 May

Lerici is the most serene of the Italian Riviera resorts, and Shelley's house on the waterfront is desolate no longer. A plaque upon it records the tragedy of the poet's drowning, and Mary's poignant watch upon the balcony. Shelley's body was burnt on the beach at Viareggio, some twenty-five miles to the south, where it had been washed ashore.

Undoubtedly Tuscany beyond Siena is the most beautiful of all lands anywhere – it is, at the moment, every inch of it laden with flowers: then there are nightingales: but it is the hills, – no, I will not describe for your annoyance. what is to me the loveliest, the most sympathetic, and I may say Virgilian of countries; for its years since we read Virgil together and you very properly told me not to write a word about landscape or art either.

And the peasants are infinitely the nicest of our kind – oh how much preferable to the Sands, the Smyths, the Logans! My Italian lands me in all kinds of wayside conversations, as we generally lunch under olives, beside streams with frogs barking. Why didn't you come? I should have thought the pictures very good at Siena – and then I like the old maids one meets: but the truth is this is only a discovery – we must come and settle at Fabbria [in Tuscany], a little farm we found, for ever and ever. . . . Yesterday we went to a place where I shall be buried, if bones can walk – that is, Monte Oliveto; oh oh oh – Cypresses, square tanks, oxen, and not big bony hills, little velvety hills – and the monastery: and as hot as August. But I wont deny that we've had some very cold days, and some violent tempests, one at Volterra for example – all because a peasant woman whose vines were perishing, came in and offered 2 candles for rain – which promptly came.

Letter to Vanessa Bell, 17 May

Monte Oliveto Maggiore, the fourteenth-century Benedictine monastery near Siena, is now one of Tuscany's great tourist destinations, but apart from the oxen (long tractorised) has changed very little. When in 1992 I told some English pilgrims there that I was following in the footsteps of Virginia Woolf, one of them said that those Bloomsbury sort of people should not have been allowed inside.

Today [near Siena] we saw the most beautiful of views & the melancholy man. The view was like a line of poetry that makes itself; the shaped hill, all flushed with reds & greens; the elongated lines, cultivated every inch; old, wild, perfectly said, once & for all: & I walked up to a group & said What is that village? It called itself [. . .]; & the woman with the blue eyes said wont you come to my house & drink? She was famished for talk. Four or five of them buzzed round us, & I made a Ciceronian speech, about the beauty of the country. But I have no money to travel with, she said, wringing her hands. We would not go to her house – or cottage on the side of the hill, & shook hands; hers were dusty; she wanted to keep them from me; but we all shook hands, & I wished we had gone to her house, in the loveliest of all landscapes. Then, lunching by the river among the ants, we met the melancholy man. He had five or six little fish in his hands, which he had caught in his hands. We said it was very beautiful country; & he said no, he preferred the town. He had been to Florence; no, he did not like the country. He wanted to travel, but had no money: worked at some village; no he did not like the country, he repeated, with his gentle cultivated voice; no theatres, no pictures, only perfect beauty. I gave him 2 cigarettes; at first he refused, then offered us his 6 or 7 little fish. But we could not cook them at Siena, we said. No, he agreed; & so we parted.

Diary, 13 May

This should be all description – I mean of the little pointed green hills; & the white oxen, & the poplars, & the cypresses, & the sculptured shaped infinitely musical, flushed green land from here [Siena] to Abbazia [Abbey of Sant' Antimo] – that is where we went today; & couldn't find it, & asked one after another of the charming tired peasants, but none had been 4 miles beyond their range, until we came to the stone breaker, & he knew. He could not stop work to come with us, because the inspector was coming tomorrow. And he was alone, alone, all day with no one to talk to. So was the aged Maria at the Abbazio. And she mumbled & slipped her words, as she showed us into the huge bare stone building; mumbled & mumbled, about the English – how beautiful they were. Are you a Contessa? she asked me. But she didnt like Italian country either. They seem stinted, dried up; like grasshoppers, & with the manners of impoverished gentle people; sad, wise, tolerant, humorous. There was the man with the mule. He let the mule gallop away down the road. We are welcome, because we might talk; they draw round & discuss us after we're gone. Crowds of gentle kindly boys & girls always come about us, & wave & touch their hats. And nobody looks at the view – except us – at the Euganean, bone white, this evening: then there's a ruddy red farm or two; & light islands swimming here & there in the sea of shadow – for it was very showery – then there are the black stripes of cypresses round the farms; like fur ridges; & the poplars, & the streams & the nightingales singing & sudden gusts of orange blossom; & white alabaster oxen, with swinging chins – great flaps of white leather hanging under their noses – & infinite emptiness, loneliness, silence: never a new house, or a village; but only the vineyards & the olive trees, where they have always been. The hills go pale blue, washed very sharp & soft on the sky; hill after hill . . .

Diary, 15 May

Virginia had been reading too much Shelley ('Many a green isle needs must lie/ In the deep wide sea of misery'): the Euganean

Hills are 150 miles away, near Padua. The 'huge bare' Roman-esque Abbey of Sant' Antimo, in its exquisite valley near Montalcino, has been sympathetically brought to life again, and now houses five Benedictine monks, besides a multitude of swallows, pigeons and hooded crows nesting in its brickwork.

Scenes of Rome, *1927*

I am sure Rome is the city where I shall come to die – a few months before death however, for obviously the country round it is far the loveliest in the world. I dont myself care so much for the melodramatic mountains here, which go the colour of picture postcards at sunset; but outside Rome it is perfection – smooth, suave, flowing, classical, with the sea on one side, hills on the other, a flock of sheep here, and an olive grove. There I shall come to die.

Letter to Vanessa Bell, 9 April

Undoubtedly I shall settle here – it surpasses all my expectations: It is a holiday today and all sights are shut so we have done nothing but sit in the gardens and stroll over to St Peters. I dont know why one feels it to be so much superior to other cities – partly the colour I suppose. It is a perfect day; all the flowers are just out, there are great bushes of azalea set in the paths; Judas trees, cypresses, lawns, statues, among which go wandering the Italian nurses in their primrose and pink silks with their veils and laces and instead of being able to read Proust, as I had meant . . . I find myself undulating like a fish in and out of leaves and flowers and swimming round a vast earthenware jar which changes from orange red to leaf green – It is incredibly beautiful – oh and there's St Peters in the distance; and people sitting on the parapet, all very distinguished, the loveliest women in Europe, with little proud heads; – but you will not attach any sense to all this.

Letter to Vanessa Bell, 21 April

We rambled over the Campagna on Sunday. I suppose France is all right, and England is all right, but I have never seen anything so beautiful as this is. Figure us sitting in hot sunshine on the doorstep of a Roman ruin in a field with hawk coloured archways against a clear green grape coloured sky, silvery with mountains in the back ground. Then on the other side nothing but the Campagna, blue and green, with an almond coloured farm, with oxen and sheep, and more ruined arches, and blocks of marble fallen on the grass, and immense sword like aloes, and lovers curled up among the broken pots. Nemi perhaps you have seen. We lunched at a restaurant hung above the lake, which is almost round, very deep, with Roman ships sunk in it, and of the colour first of olive trees and then of emeralds. It was rather cloudy so the colour was always changing very slowly, and round the lake was a little path with horses and goats. We went down after lunch and found wild cyclamen and marble lapped by the water. Dear, dear, and then one goes and sits in a basement in Bloomsbury!

Letter to Vanessa Bell, 26 April

In the following year the lake at Nemi was temporarily drained, and the two ceremonial galleys found on its bottom were recovered, restored and housed in a museum: but they were destroyed by fire in 1944, allegedly by soldiers of the retreating German Army. Otherwise almost everything Virginia says about Rome will be recognisable to visitors today – and they can still stay at the luxurious hotel, the Hassler at the top of the Spanish Steps (in those days called the Hassler-New York) in which she and Leonard indulged themselves.

Spain

Eighteen years separated Virginia Woolf's two visits to Spain. On the first journey, when she was twenty-three, she travelled with her brother Adrian by sea to Portugal, and then by train to Andalusia. She recorded the trip, which she evidently did not much enjoy, in what seems to me the most naïve of her travel diaries.

Down to Andalusia
Diary, 1905

The night was more comfortable than I expected. We did not undress, but lay in a kind of sofa, with a pillow, which was quite soft. All day we travelled; arriving, at Badajoz on the Spanish frontier at 8. And so through Estremadura, & Andalusia – splendid names! But the country is not beautiful; for the most part, flat, & treeless, & the sun was hot. The train stopped at every village on the way. In the afternoon we came to wilder & more interesting country, & with very few roads & houses, & great views. At 8.30 we reached Seville, drove to Hotel Roma, had a gloomy dinner & to bed.

8 April

*The hotel, of the second rank, was in the Plaza del Duque de la
Victoria, and later became the Venecia, the Roma having started
up somewhere else.*

We began to explore Seville this morning. First to the
Cathedral, which looms everywhere. It is vast. That is the
first impression. I dont very much care for such elephantine
beauty – but it is fine . . . In the afternoon we took a carriage & drove for an hour in the gardens which are lovely,
though somewhat faded & out of repair, like everything
else. The streets are very narrow, cobbled, with no pavement to walk on. Trams bad & not easy to get. It is a difficult
town to find ones way about in.

9 April

Woke this morning under my mosquito curtains – which
the beasts merely laugh at – to find, firstly the maid carrying on a long & emphatic speech in Spanish – & 2ndly a
rain of pure English blood pouring outside . . . Out in a clear
space to the Giralda, which is the Cathedral Tower, from
which we gazed over Seville; a small town it looks from
that height, soon dwindling off into fields. White houses
with brown roofs for the most part. The rain was such that
we sat a long time in the Cathedral – which is not really
beautiful, though certainly impressive – in the same way
that a steep cliff or a bottomless well is. In the afternoon we
'did' Alcázar, a splendid gilt & mosaic Moorish building – a
sight again which does not charm me.

10 April

At 7 happily I woke, & we dressed for 7.30 breakfast, &
without much regret left the hotel at 8. We travelled all day
long, & changed twice. We had to indulge in things called
Berliner – coupes for 2, as all the 1sts were crowded. But on
the whole the journey was more comfortable than last

time. We got finally to a wild hilly region – the Sierra Nev-
adas in the midst of which Granada is set. Here, at 8.15 we
arrived & were driven by 4 mules to the top of the high hill
on which the Washington Irving stands. There we happily
found rooms, dined & to bed.

12 April

*The Washington Irving Hotel flourishes still, in the lee of the
Alhambra above the city of Granada.*

Out as usual this morning to explore. We find ourselves in
the greenest shade, as of great English trees, filtering a
Southern sun . . . Unhappily, owing to some red tape, we
had to tramp all the way to the town to get cards of admis-
sion, which took some time. The gardens are worth a good
deal. They are very hot & fragrant, all in little inlaid terraces
like an Italian garden, with cool summer houses where one
may rest & look over the city to the snow mountains
beyond. In the afternoon we were taken over the Alhambra by the guide, a gorgeous Moorish palace & within
battered yellow walls.

13 April

This morning we 'did' the town, which mainly consists
of the Cathedral – a dull florid building, very ornate,
containing only one thing that interested me – the tomb
of Ferdinand & Isabella . . . After dinner A.&.I with two
people – father & daughter who have made friends with us
– went up to a court of the Alhambra and saw the gipseys
dance.

14 April

At 6.30 this morning we breakfasted, & at 7 left in the Bus.
We had a long tiresome journey, as usual, changing &c; at 9
we arrived at a place called Amonhon where we were to

sleep. There being, we were told, a 'good second class hotel'. Making all allowances for Spanish hotels as we did, we were not prepared for a little white cottage, a kind of public house, by the side of a desert & a Moorish castle, where we had to spend the night. There was one room, so we lay in our clothes on the bed, & managed to sleep a little till 5.30 when we had to pay 3 pesetas, & our train started at 6.

16 April

I have been unable to identify this uncomfortable place, and suspect that Virginia got its name wrong. See below for more.

We travelled till 12.30, & then stopped at Badajoz – where we had to wait 6 hours – a very dreary time, as we were sleepy, & miserable – the town hot & dirty, & we had nothing to do. We tried to find something to look at, & listened to a comic performance in the Cathedral, which I likened to the singing of old country songs by half tipsey farmers. The Cathedral might perhaps be fine; but they have defaced it with glass. At 7. or so we happily left Badajoz, got an empty first class, which took us without change to Lisbon. We eat some hard boiled eggs & slept fairly well stretched on the seats.

17 April

An Andalusian Inn
Essay in the Guardian, *19 July 1905*

From Virginia Woolf's unsatisfactory first journey to Spain there survives one of her very few set-piece travel essays. The inn it describes is unidentified, but is evidently the cottage at 'Amonhon' which she records in her diary entry for 16 April above.

Hotel-keepers are apparently subject to that slight and amiable obliquity of the moral sense which goes by the name of loyalty. Thus, when we asked whether we should find good quarters for a night's rest at a certain little country town in Andalusia where we had to sleep we were assured that the hotel there was good. Not, of course, a first-class establishment such as the palatial building in which we stood, but, nevertheless, a good second-class inn, where we should be made comfortable and provided with beds of the cleanest. At half past nine, then, when after a long day's loitering through the country the train finally came to a stop and announced its intention of going no further, the hotel-keeper's word sounded comfortable in our ears. We should be content with little, we reflected, and during the last stages of the journey, as the orthodox dinner hour passed uncelebrated and the wick which swam in the oil-lamp committed suicide – and its life had not been happy – we dwelt much upon the terms of this recommendation and the good second-class inn became an epitome of all that is desirable in life. Here we should meet with a simple-hearted welcome; we pictured the innkeeper and his wife coming out to greet us, eager to take our bundles and our wraps – bustling about to prepare our rooms and catch the fowl who was to make our dinner. For the night's rest between clean and scented sheets the plain but delicious dinner and the excellent breakfast before our early start they would ask some ridiculously small sum. We should be made to feel that silver is a most vulgar coin in which to pay such hospitality, and that that noble virtue – long dead among the innkeepers of our own country – still flourishes in Spain.

In thoughts like these we passed the time till the train had reached the station where we would be rewarded for all our joltings and fatigues. It was a little disconcerting to find that the porters, at any rate, were evidently surprised that two travellers with heavy luggage should be deposited on the platform at this time of night. The inevitable crowd came running to stare at us, and gaped when we produced the careful arrangement of Spanish words in which we signified our desire for an inn. A sentence in a conversation-book is something of the nature of an extinct monster in a museum: only the specially initiated can tell you that it is related to the live animal. It was at once obvious that our specimen was hopelessly extinct, and, further, a terrible doubt insinuated itself that it was the nature of what we asked as much as the language in which we asked it that was unintelligible. At length, after much Spanish, French, and English had clashed unprofitably, it dawned upon the natives that we did not speak their language, and the powers of gesticulation were tried upon us. Presently an official appeared who informed us that he could speak French. Our request for an hotel was joyfully translated into that language. 'The train goes no further to-night,' answered the interpreter. 'We know that, and therefore we wish to sleep here,' we said. 'To-morrow morning at 5.30.' 'But to-night, an hotel,' we insisted. The gentleman who spoke French produced a pencil with an air of resignation, and wrote large and very black the figures 5 and 30. We shrugged our shoulders, and vociferated 'hotel' first in French and then in three different kinds of Spanish. The crowd had by this time made a complete circle round us, and every one was translating for the benefit of his neighbour. We then bethought us of a Spanish dictionary, which had consistently refused to be left behind, and the Spanish equivalent for the English word 'hotel' was found and emphasised with a forefinger. As many heads as could be pressed together gazed blankly at the spot thus indicated, and the interpreter was struck by a brilliant idea. He lost the place and searched feverishly for a word of his own among the Ss and the Zs. We helped him to the Spanish department of the dictionary, and left him to prolonged, but, as it turned out, fruitless researches.

Meanwhile we repeated our solitary word in the chance that it might somewhere fall upon fertile soil. At every utterance a buzz of good Spanish rose from the crowd; finally, when we were trying to define hotel with an umbrella, a small old man forced himself upon our notice. To the inevitable question he answered by laying his hand upon his breast and bowing profoundly. We asked him three times in succession, and he always answered in the same way, as though in his solitary person he combined all the qualities we needed. Public opinion seemed to be unanimous that we should accept him as the representative of dinner and bed, and a few last attempts at the Spanish for 'inn' were answered by hands stretched in his direction. To settle the matter he gripped us by the arm and drew us outside the station to the edge of a sandy desert grown with tufts of reeds and lighted by a large moon. On one side was a steep hill, crowned by a Moorish castle, and at a little distance we saw a solitary cottage. The choice apparently lay between the two, and neither seemed precisely what we had expected. We looked at the old man, and observed not without relief that he was both old and small. One of our doubts, at any rate, was soon at an end, for it was clear that the white cottage was to be our lodging, and that the hotel-keeper at Granada had the imagination of an artist. We were shown into a room where a lamp burnt, and where several men and women sat round a fire drinking and talking. There was a pause, in which several eyes inspected us at their leisure, and we were led into an ante-room, in whose honour that word 'hotel' had been applied to the cottage. There was a bed and a canvas partition to serve as door, water to wash in, if we chose to keep up that respectable farce, and a candle in case we wished for light. Food, it was clear, must be sought at the station; and we were by no means unwilling to go out into the fresh air again. When at the hour of eleven we were tired of the Spanish desert, and the Moorish castle, and the conversation of the gentleman who could speak French, but did not think it essential to understand that language, we returned to the inn and began what promised to be a somewhat weary vigil. The company sat late and talked loud. Scraps of vehement Spanish penetrated the canvas partition, and somehow seemed to be concerned with us. Spanish is a fierce and bloodthirsty language when heard under these conditions. The figure of our small friend with his perpetual bows and finger laid on his breast became towards midnight of a very sinister aspect; we remembered his ominous silence, his persistent determination that we should be parted from our luggage. Country people of honest conscience, we reflected, should have been in bed long before this. The only precaution possible to us was to stand the solitary chair on its hind legs against the door. That must have had a strangely composing effect upon our minds, for, thus fortified against the murderous assault which we expected, we fell asleep in our clothes, and dreamed that we had found the Spanish word for 'inn'.

The sound that finally awoke us at half past four in the morning was certainly an assault upon the door; but when we cautiously looked out there was no one more hostile than the peasant woman with a basin of goat's milk in her hands.

Through the Sierra Nevada, *1923*

In 1923 Virginia returned to Spain with her husband Leonard, in their first foreign journey since their honeymoon. They went to visit the writer Gerald Brenan at his house in the remote Alpujarra, in the Sierra Nevada. The journey was made by train, by bus, and finally by mule from Granada.

. . . This wrinkled red and white screen [the Sierra Nevada] is found to consist of stones, olive trees, goats, asphodels, irises, bushes, ridges, shelves, clumps, tufts, and hollows innumerable, indescribable, unthinkable. The mind's contents break into short sentences. It is hot; the old man; the frying pan; it is hot; the image of the Virgin; the bottle of wine; it is time for lunch; it is only half-past twelve; it is hot. And then over and over again come all those objects – stones, olives, goats, asphodels, dragon-flies, irises, until by some trick of the imagination they run into phrases of command, exhortation, and encouragement such as befit soldiers marching, sentinels on lonely nights, and leaders of great battalions. But must one give up the struggle? Must one relinquish the game? Yes, for the clouds are drifting across the pass; mules mind not what they carry; mules never stumble; they know the way. Why not leave everything to them?

Riders, as night comes on (and the pass was very misty), seem to be riding out of life towards some very enticing prospect, while the four legs of their beasts carry on all necessary transactions with the earth. Riders are at rest; on they go, and on and on. And, they muse, what does it all matter; and what harm can come to a good man (behold two priests stepping out of the drizzle, bowing and disappearing) in life or after death? And then, since a fox has crossed the path, which is on turf and must be nearly at the top of the mountain, how strangely it seems as if they were riding in England, a long day's journey, hundreds of years ago, and the danger is over, and they see the lights of the inn, and the hostess comes into the courtyard and bids them sit round the fire while she cooks dinner, which they do, half-dreaming, while clumsy boys and girls with red flowers pass and repass in the background, and the mother suckles her baby, and the old man, who never speaks, breaks tufts from the brushwood and throws them on the fire, which blazes up, and the whole company stares.

But, good heavens! One never knows what days follow what nights. Good heavens again! 'Don Fernando had a passion for pigeon pie, and so kept pigeons up here' – on his roof, that is, from which one has this astonishing, this strange, this disturbing view of the Alpujarras. 'He died last summer in Granada.' Did he, indeed? It is the light, of course; a million razor-blades have shaved off the bark and the dust, and out pours pure colour; whiteness from fig trees; red and green and again white from the enormous, the humped, the everlasting landscape. But listen to the sounds on the roof – first the fluttering pigeons; then water rushing; then an old man crying chickens for sale; then a donkey braying in the valley far below. Listen; and as one listens this random life begins to be issued from the heart of a village which has faced the African coast with a timeless and aristocratic endurance for a thousand years. But how say this (as one descends from the blaze) to the Spanish peasant woman who bids one enter her room, with its lilies and its washing, and smiles and looks out of the window as if she too had looked for a thousand years?

Essay in the Nation & Athenaeum, *5 May*

After this rough journey through the wilds the Woolfs spent an agreeable week in the village of Yegen, which is now easily reached by excellent roads, and where Brenan's house is marked by a plaque. Virginia however wrote nothing about their stay, beyond describing Brenan variously as 'very nice', 'slightly blurred', 'a mad Englishman who does nothing but read French and eat grapes', and as having 'some phantasmagoric resemblance to Shelley'. (Brenan on the other hand wrote that Virginia Woolf, though an imaginative genius, was so tied to the Bloomsbury set that she 'could only throw distant and uneasy glances outside it').

The Woolfs ended their acquaintance with Spain by travelling down to Alicante and thence along the coast into France.

Here [in Alicante] it is always fine, always indolent; one drinks coffee, listens to the Band, ships come in, old men spit; last night I did not sleep till 4, because of bugs. At 4 Leonard extricated a camel shaped lump of purple tissue from the hairs of my blanket. It burst with an odious smell into thick blood. So do not expect much continuity, cogency, or clarity from me. I am sitting in a Spanish gentleman's Club, to which travellers are admitted. There is only one old gentleman and his spittoon in the midst of a vast yellow chamber, set tight round the walls with wicker chairs, and in the midst breadths of white marble and vistas of billiard tables and courtyards and arum lilies beyond.

We are waiting for a ship to take us to Barcelona, but owing to the feast of the conception of the Virgin the ship remains at Carthagena, and so we grill here, watching the ships, listening to the band as I say. But we have been among the eternal snows [at Yegen], on mule back, and crouched over olive wood fires with deformed Catalans at midnight . . . In short, I cannot even begin to chatter.

Letter to Mary Hutchinson, 18 April

Greece

Virginia Woolf's attitudes to Greece were conventional among English people of her class and period. She came from a classically educated family, she had taken pains to study ancient Greek, and during her two journeys to the country she visited many of the most celebrated sites of antiquity. Later she extended her view, as by then was fashionable, to embrace Byzantium.

On the Grand Tour I
Journal, September–October 1906

Virginia Woolf's first Greek visit was made with her sister Vanessa, her two brothers and their friend Violet Dickinson, and was partly spoilt by Vanessa's repeated illnesses. The three women entered Greece by sea from Italy, at Patras, the men met them there, and all five proceeded on the Grand Tour.

Patras like most sea ports is cosmopolitan, & very garrulous. We saw men in skirts & gaiters however. Turks, Albanians & Montenegrins scattered about among a humdrum crowd. But in the evening, having heard meanwhile a plaintive Greek song we interpreted the words generously – We left for Olympia in a great first class carriage which we had naturally to ourselves. Now it was evening, & the bloom on the hills shone purple, & the sea turned its innermost heart to the light; it was a heart of the deepest blue. On the other side of us was a screen of hills, sudden & steep & incessant, as though the earth had nothing better to do than throw up impatient little mounds. The look of the place thus is fiery & somewhat fragile, for the lines are all very spare & emphatic. No fat pastures & woods cushion the surface: but on the plain the earth was thick with dwarf vines, stooping with pyramids of fruit. You saw baskets heaped with grapes at the stations: Stafeelé stafeelé – I cried – & brought great bunches to the door.

The stations were many; we stopped that is at sheds where, by the light of a lantern, men were drinking wine, with their horses tied to a stake; as the railway curved the whistle shrieked a continual warning, for the line is like a modest little road, & in truth the train would do no great damage to a flock of goats.

The pediments of the temple [at Olympia] line the two sides of the museum; but we wont write guide book – There is the Apollo. He looks over his shoulder – seems to look across & above the centuries. He is straight & serene but there he has a human mouth & chin, ready to quiver or to smile. So might a Greek boy have looked, stripped, in the sun. And there are other noble fragments, somewhat broadly chiselled, because they stood on a height; the hair is a smooth band of stone; the drapery graved in rigid lines. Ah but the beauty!

Then you come to the separate temple, where the Hermes stands still, so lightly & with such a spring in his step that you expect him to turn & go. There, I think, you have the God; for he looks out & away, as though some serene vistas in the far Heaven drew his gaze.

So we pile words; but it is a pretence. You must see him, & let the eye spring like a creature set free along those curves & hollows; for it has secretly craved such beauty!

You dont know, till you satisfy it, how much it has craved.
And the stone – if you call it stone – seems also acquiescent
to the sculptors hand: it is almost liquid, of the colour of
alabaster, & of the solidity of marble. There is a beautiful
polished foot which you may stroke with your own soft
flesh. The Germans have supplied plaster legs. Let us note
it. If only it had been possible to stand the statue in the air!
Cold stone needs that background. The theatre is – once
more we might quote the Guidebook: for our purposes it is
simply a flat circle of grass, scattered with innumerable
fragments of stone. There are broken pillars of all sizes, &
tiles, stones, lion heads, inscriptions; it is like, perhaps, a
very disorderly pagan graveyard. But you may trace certain
temples, & the course of the race ground. Still this is not
what the vagrant mind dwells on most; there was thyme
growing by the pillars, & fine grass. And there were little
hills tufted with delicate green trees all round; & the
Alpheus [river] passing on one side.

*Olympia is now a greater tourist attraction than ever, thanks to
the appeal of the revived Olympic Games (in 1906 only three of the
modern Olympiads had yet been held, in Athens, Paris and St
Louis). A new museum now houses all the greatest of its treasures,
including the Hermes of Praxitiles. They were cyclamens that were
growing by the pillars, when I was there.*

. . . In a short time I was ascending the Acro Corinth [the
fortress of ancient Corinth] on a grey pony; you climb a
precipice, & bask on the top beneath a Turkish fortification.
You see Salamis & some of the most famous lands of the
world beneath you. The colour of the country seen thus in
great spaces from a height is that of tawny sand; it might be
a desert, save for some squares of thin green. And you see
Corinth lying by the edge of the gulf. But it was not a day
for seeing far, & it was very hot, & I had spent the night in
pursuits of another kind. So we drove back again, & I confess that the pleasantest part of the expedition was due to

the fact that our coachman was also a vine owner; & as we drove through his land, hospitality & a desire to see how his crop was doing, made him beg us to dismount & taste his produce. And so we had the experience for the first time of sitting on the ground & eating grapes from the tree in the open air. The skins were warmed through, & that made the globe of juice within all the sweeter & more cool. Grapes for nothing!

There is a motor road now to the triple gateway of the Acro Corinth, but the vineyards still lie all around.

We travelled down to Nauplia by steamer. And if this steamer had not smelt, & if it had not had the cruel consequences of smelling ships, no voyage could have been more pleasant. The sea was only broken by the leap of the Dolphins; we passed so near the shore that we could see the little villages folded among the hills; now & then we stopped in the harbour of some more important place. The towns built pyramids up the hills; & altogether you had as fair & various a view of the Greek coast as you could wish. There are not many towns, & the land is very bleak & stony. You could not imagine a walk in such country; nor, with the level sun upon it, was it really a beautiful land. It was too fierce, too precipitous; &, in that light, too much of the colour of bare bone. We had a small company on deck who, like most of the poor people who are not inn keepers, seemed courteous & cheerful. There was a small boy for instance who gave us a lemon in return for our egg, & kissed our hands when we left. It was a long journey, for we crossed the gulf, & the dents on the map became deep bays, & we slackened steam, & went slowly on our way till 9.30 when we anchored . . .

We drove . . . today . . . to Epidauros. The country when you penetrate within the bare line of the coast, is strange &

beautiful. There are long red roads, that pass through red fields rough with stones, & planted with twisted olive trees, or with dwarf vines; there are incessant hills, but inland they are covered with little green bushes, & the high folds among which we drove today reminded us again of Cornwall. Oddly enough the narrow streets of Athens reminded us of St Ives. Three sad jades drew our carriage the 20 miles; We passed many flocks of goats, many sumpter mules, many carts laden with wine skins. But there were only two small villages, & there was no sign of our snug English civilisation. Epidauros . . . lies on flat land beneath a circle of hills.

There is the great theatre, so perfect that we could sit in its upper seats & look down upon the stage & hear the voice of one speaking there as in the best of halls. And the grey seats scooped out of the hillside, with wide air & country all round are as noble a theatre as could be had. Ruins of Roman Houses, Temples of Asclepios – Tholos – are scattered innumerable. It needs learning to see anything but chips of stone. And in the museum chaos is still more chaotic: they are fitting temples together, hammering the old stone into the right shape.

The place is very lovely; although you must leave the ruins for bed. It is so wide & harmonious, & the country is all grouped round decorously.

When I was at Epidauros in 1992 the acoustics of the theatre, said to be the most perfect of them all, were being demonstrated by an elderly Scandinavian lady and a young male companion, twice her height, who together sang a melodious Finnish folk song among the ruins. 'Viva Europa!' I cried when they finished, but nobody took much notice.

There never was a sight, I think less manageable [than Mycenae]; it travels through all the chambers of the brain, wakes odd memories & imaginations; forecasts a remote future; retells a remote past. And all the while it is – let me write it down – but a great congeries of ruined houses, on a hill side. So you may see the outline of a wall in an English farmyard, tenanted 60 years ago by a serf; these were built let us say one thousand years before Christ; they have certainly lain in ruins since the year – was it four hundred & sixty? But among these houses, you come across something far more definite; an αγορα, a tomb, a palace with a flight of steps. The whole hill top is crowded with dead stones; & yet they are not dead. The tracery is too emphatic: the mark is too deeply scored.

The imagination does assert again & again, as you walk, that the place is crowded & compact; it is true there is little to see & nothing to hear. But the tremendous stones are not to be ignored, & the two lions, which guard the gate, do still consciously admit you to something august which is beyond. I tremble to write of the classics, because that might savour of the perfunctory impulse of the guide book; but the taste of Homer was in my mouth. Indeed, this is the pearl of seeing things here; the words of the poets begin to sing & embody themselves. This is no pretence, moreover, as it may so easily be at home, in a London room; it needs no effort; but if statues & marble are solid to the touch, so, simply, are words resonant to the ear.

I picked up an earthenware handle with its little pattern still brightly stamped on it; & once more it was easy to believe that the whole crest was packed with unbroken litter, of the prehistoric city. The circumference of the town is not large; but then every foots pace of it is set with stone, & it must have been a populous town; so closely occupied because the outer world was vast and lonely. How far history, or mythology, warrants me, I do not know; but I conceived that here was a single spot of intense, & brilliantly painted life, girt in by great wastes of desert land. The people had not come yet. And I conceived that the Kings & people of Mycenae lived a decorous life, strictly ordered, as the town itself is graven in distinct divisions. They were simple & austere, as tho' conscious that they lived with a great eye upon them, an isolated people, adventuring alone; but in the limits of their town they lived with much ornament & decoration: the king wore purple robes, & his limbs shone with beaten gold. They had many festivals, & when it was summer they marched down the hill side in ceremonial procession, glittering in dyed clothing & ornament & gold, with offerings outstretched in their hands. The valley was kindled by the sun, & they threaded it like bright summer flies. And the thyme smelt sweet as ambrosia. And in the evening they were all gathered in order in their courts, & perhaps a great beacon burnt; in case man or God beheld it.

And yet after all, they may have thought many of our thoughts, & felt many of our passions. Certainly they beheld the same hillside, grey with rock; ominous & melancholy I thought it, in the September light.

It was thirty years, almost to the month, since Heinrich Schliemann (1822-1890) had begun the excavations at Mycenae which were to make the name of the place universally known, and which satisfied him (if not everyone else) that a historical Agamemnon was buried within the Lion Gate. The gold, silver and ivory objects he found there were to remain the richest archaeological treasure ever found until the opening of Tutankhamun's tomb in 1922 – 'all the museums of the world taken together,' Schliemann exulted, 'do not have one-fifth as much.'

Virginia and her party made a detour from the usual tourist route to visit the island of Evvoia (Euboea), where the Noel family had, since 1832, owned the estate called Achmetaga, at modern Prokopion. The daughter of the family, Irene, was a friend of theirs.

At five this morning we stood before the Inn at Calchis waiting for our carriage, while the rain poured. Even so we could see the boats, drifting down the current, & the great steamers gliding among them. In the sun it would have been beautiful; in the mud it was vague & comfortless as a dream. At last our horses came, & we mounted to drive 32

206

miles to Achmetaga. Now you have to travel along a plain, & to climb a mountain, & to curl like a langorous serpent round the front of the precipice; & then you must descend, as tortuously into the valley, & drive among steep hill sides covered with trees, & the trees cluster thick in the valley, over the dry bed of the stream. We proposed last night to go straight on, driving all night, to reach Achmetaga this morning, but the driver said no: it was dangerous. So we amused ourselves by counting the number of times we should have fallen over the broken parapet, or stepped right in to the great hole in the road, or fallen headlong down the precipice; for surely as we narrowly escaped these dangers by day, we should have been snared for a certainty by night. A Scotch mist was quite dark enough. We baited our horses at an inn on the way, which we might then examine curiously. It was a barn, with a wall separating it into two rooms. One was stable, the other bedroom dining room living room &c. for husband & wife & children. We looked in through the iron grating, & saw the woman in a corner, working her distaff; she sat on a mat. The children played round her; there was a hole in the chimney, & a heap of ashes on the floor, & bread & onions stood on planks. Here was England in the 14th Century; it was dark & probably smelly: tins & plates gleamed in corners. A man like a serf brought us bread & water.

But we pressed on, & at 2 o'clock found ourselves entering a village – almost the first we had passed. There were hovels heaped up in a valley, & a square white house raised among them. Shutters & terraces showed that we had come to our goal; & so we dismounted & found ourselves in an English drawing room. English drawing rooms it is true are generally more richly furnished; There are carpets on the floors, & many chairs. This room suggested that its windows were perpetually open, & as its owners lived out of doors there was not much need for any decoration but what was cool & simple. Still, however open & ricketty, the place had the effect of making you feel that you had come to the genuine living place at last, after skimming a factitious exterior for a long time. Here people lived, not merely stayed. And this impression remains; indeed for the first time Greece becomes an articulate human place, homely & familiar, instead of a splendid surface. We walked out down a lane that might have been in England – for it had a hedge, & was muddy, to see an encampment of Wallachian shepherds . . . They are a nomad people, tending sheep, who roam in the mountains all the summer, & pitch their tents, or rather their huts, in the winter . . . We were asked . . . to go inside their huts. They are made of boughs, & the dead leaves serve for lining to the roof. A family of twelve children lived here; brown & sallow, gentle & communicative. They shook hands – the women were weaving cloth, in an outer court; & inside was the sleeping place of the family. They live, presumably, in the open air; we peered round, & tried, not very successfully, to imagine the whole life, built on such a foundation. But this needs more imagination than any other feat of archaeology; for mud huts belong to the dark ages. The people did not look robust or fierce; one or two women had notably fine faces, aquiline & expressive. Then we tramped some way over the estate; & this would be a dull record, but all the time, somehow – I can't define it – you felt the place arrange itself in its natural order, & this was something beautiful. Here were the olive groves – here they dug a trench – here come all the village people, trooping home from work with their salutations, prompt & respectful. Miss Noel knew each by name; each spoke to her. Now this seemed to give what was wanting to Greece before; & it is a very essential part of it. The people use the same plough that they did in the days of Homer, says Mrs Noel, & though the races have changed, their lives cannot be much different; the earth changes but little.

Achmetaga stands on a flight of steps, with its garden in terraces; & a view far & wide to distant mountains, framed by tall trees. The garden like the house, is somehow rather ramshackle & bare; a group of women sat this morning picking walnuts from their shells on the lawn.

Meanwhile all the government of the village it seemed was transacted in the house. The nurse came for her medicines, the servants for their orders, strange figures kept walking in at the door to ask for treatment or advice. No one seemed to have any precise calling, & yet everyone seemed able & willing to do something. The groom wanted to know what soup we would have for dinner; & also he would lend a hand in the farm. Or that was my impression; the place was full of simple garrulous creatures, eager as children to be directed to their tasks, eager as children to stay & chatter with their mistress.

Miss Noel was presently to marry Philip Baker, an English Quaker politician, to Virginia's displeasure, and their son, Francis Noel-Baker, now owns Achmetaga. The family's presence there for 160 years has been a tumultuous saga, but the house, though it was partly burned down by the Italian soldiery during the Second World War, remains much as Virginia describes it, except that the garden is far from ramshackle. In the visitors' book, which I examined in 1992 over a glass of the Noel-Bakers' delectable Achmetaga Retsina, Virginia Stephen's signature shares a page with La Bande des Anamites, enigmatically identified simply as 'troupe de Miss Irène.'

There were many stories told us by the Noels which might be copied here. How for instance it is necessary to bribe the best doctor in Athens with the present of a pig before he will sign your nurses certificate – how, in short all classes have their price; how all Greeks lie, how all Greeks are dirty, ignorant, & unstable as water.

And considering that Mr. Noel has lived among them – as he was born among them – for some fifty years not only do his words carry weight, but it is the kind of weight that is absolute. It would have been so easy, in such a length of time with such associations, to have grown to love the people, so that a stranger hinting at their faults would have been driven back 'Not a bit of it – I know the people'. But as it is, he does know the people & this is his knowledge.

Like a shifting layer of sand these loosely composed tribes of many different peoples lie across Greece; calling themselves Greek indeed, but bearing the same kind of relation to the old Greek that their tongue does to his. For the language they talk is divided from the language that some few of them can write as widely as that again is divided from the speech of Plato. The spoken language because it has not been fixed by grammar or spelling, twists itself afresh on each tongue. The peasants drop syllables, & slur vowels so that as proficient a speaker as Miss Noel could not undertake to write down the words that ran so swiftly fr. her tongue. Nor could she either read or write the Greek of the newspapers; & still less could she read the Greek of the Classics. So you must look upon Modern Greek as the impure dialect of a nation of peasants, just as you must look upon the modern Greeks as a nation of mongrel element & a rustic beside the classic speech of pure bred races.

They arrived at Athens after dark on 16 September.

When day broke we all went to our windows, & saw that a great crag of rock surged out of the darkness, tawny & cleft with shadows, upon which two groups of columns, one tawny as the rock itself, the other white & fragile, were established. Indeed on the edge of the rock there were more columns, but the dark columns we knew were the Crown & Queen of the place, the Parthenon herself.

When you are close up to them, you see that the Parthenon is far the largest of the temples; & you see also how the surface of the pillars is chipped & scarred. The ravages are terrible, but in spite of them, the Parthenon is still radiant & young. Its columns spring up like fair round limbs, flushed with health. When we saw it first however the light was so fierce that we could hardly raise our eyes to the frieze: & for all the marble scattered at ones feet – slabs of marble, drums of marble, splinters of marble seemed to flash light at us from beneath. So with a numb feeling as though our minds had been struck inarticulate by something too great for them to grasp we cooled ourselves in the museum which lies at the base of the hill. Here there is perhaps the most beautiful thing we have yet seen. The head of the boy, with braided hair which guide books call slightly archaic. But the mouth seemed freshly carved in its soft & sensitive lines only that morning. Stay though: for the stone was also immortal.

Beautiful statues have a look not seen on living faces, or but rarely, as of serene immutability, here is a type that is enduring as the earth, nay will outlast all tangible things, for such beauty is of an essence that is immortal. And this expression on a face that is otherwise young & supple makes you breathe a higher air. It is like the kiss of dawn.

We also visited the Acropolis at sunset. And when you speak of 'the colour' of the Parthenon you are simply conforming to the exigencies of language; a painter using his craft to speak by, confesses the same limitations. The Temple glows red; the whole west pediment seems kindled, as if for the first time, in the sunset opposite: it rays light & heat, while the other temples burn with a white radiance. No place seems more lusty & alive than this platform of ancient dead stone. The fat Maidens who bear the weight of the Erechtheum on their heads, stand smiling tranquil ease, for their burden is just meet for their strength. They glory in it; one foot just advanced, their hands, one conceives, loosely curled at their sides. And the warm blue sky flows into all the crevices of the marble; yet they detach themselves, & spring in to the air, with crisp edges, unblunted, & still virile & young.

But it is the Parthenon that over comes you; it is so large, & so strong, & so triumphant. You feel warmed through & through, as though you walked by some genial hearth. But perhaps the most lovely picture in it – at least it is the most detachable – is that which you receive when you stand where the great Statue [of Pallas Athene] used to stand. She looked straight through the long doorway, made by the curved lines of the columns, & saw a long slice of Attic mountain & sky & plain, & a shining strip of the sea. It is like a panel, let in to the Parthenon to complete its beauty. It is soft, & soon grows dark, though the water still gleams; then you see that the white columns are ashy pale, & the warmth of the parthenon ebbs from her.

A bell rings down below, & once more the Acropolis is left quite alone. We walked home through the clamorous streets.

To say that the scene from the Acropolis is beautiful is an easy way out of the difficulty; all the land is bloomy as a peach, with feathery purple shadows; far off the sea gleams like dull silver; up, in the sky the clouds are trembling across the dome in crimson & gold. Meanwhile the moon is just sharp enough to cleave the blue with its thin silver edge; & one star, hangs near it. The pillars on the height are rosy as dawn; then they turn creamy white & then fade altogether. In the narrow streets which climb almost to the top the lights are flaring, & you walk in a curious soft air, blue with daylight still, though the lamps are pouring yellow into it. It is still quite warm, & the atmosphere has a curiously tangible quality to it; the streets are crowded & people come swarming down them, happy & garrulous, in crowds.

The poorer people of Athens – & all the people seem poor – have a pleasant habit of lounging up here in the evening, when their work is done; just as we stroll in our parks. They sit about on classic marble, chatting & knitting; but they do not vulgarise the place as we Tourists must do; but rather make it human & familiar.

The people of Athens are, of course, no more Athenians than I am. They do not understand Greek of the age of Pericles – when I speak it. Nor are their features more classic than their speech: the Turk & the Albanian & the French – it seems – have produced a common type enough. It is dark & dusky, small of stature, & not well grown. It is true that the streets are dignified by the presence of many rustics, in their Albanian dress; the men wear thick white coats, kilts, much pleated, & long gaiters. But this you may see written in a dozen guide books. I have seen no native women who could be distinguished from an Italian woman; & indeed, you see very few women. The streets are crowded with men drinking & smoking in the open air, even, in the country, sleeping beneath the wall; but the women keep within. You generally see them leading children, or looking from an upper window, where, presumably, they work. But the mind has no difficulty in making brigands.

The modern town of Athens is like most foreign towns, so a British traveller may summarily conclude, for the roofs are of fluted brown tiles, the walls are white, & there are shutters to the windows. And so it follows that the modern town is rather fragile & gimcracky, built to flash in the sun, to bask & to bake. Then there are certain great squares where the people crowd; there are trams & there are official buildings. People chatter & shout a great deal, & jostle each other on the pavement. At noon there is a lull; everybody snores; at 4 we wake again, & begin to chatter. The liveliest scene perhaps is that of the streets at evening, when the sun has just sunk & the boats in the Piraeus have fired their guns.

Athens, as every schoolboy knows, lies in a plain; & the famous mountains stand round her – Hymettus, Lycabettus, Pentelicus – & others I daresay, whose names I have forgotten. They are grey green for the most part; but Pentelicus wears a white scar on her side, where the Greeks used to quarry marble. We started early to climb the height, for although the ascent was to be made by carriage & mule, Pentelicus is after all higher than any English mountain, & thus claimed our respect. An Athenian carriage is a most respectable vehicle, savouring somehow of the undertaker, & not at all of Greece; it is black & shabby, & is drawn by two thin horses. It looks most incongruous upon a country road stuffed with picturesque peasants, & their bags & boxes, & turkeys & goats. Yet you meet it often in this guise 'moving house' for some rustic family. It travels slowly, & it was midday when we had bargained for our horses – who were transformed to donkeys – & had dismounted at the monastery, of – I dont know what – at the foot of Pentelicus. The country is for the most part so bare & dry that these little spots, where the firs grow, & great planes, & water gushes, are exquisite – as an idyll by Theocritus. We eat our lunch in the shade of a great tree, while our donkeys grazed, & our guides lay on their elbows watching us. An aged monk came down from the hill side burdened with brushwood; another, tall & melancholy, stood at the monastery door. Then the ascent began, four of us perched on high wooden saddles, in single file, each attended by a boy or man to guide & belabour. We climbed ... a little hill in the mountain, which was paved with loose blocks of marble. Soon we had to dismount; the agony of our guides – they curst like lost souls – failed to move our steeds. It was hot & steep, & one had to leap from stone to stone, without the agility of a goat. Then we found that we were directed to a great cave, which was cool as a temple, & had some claim to fame. I forget what. And then it appeared that the guides wished to descend; pretended that they had done their duty – swore they could go no further without food, & turned our donkeys downward. This could be conveyed sufficiently by signs; our expostulations though couched in pure English – cut the air. They answered with a gabble of Greek: so it was not the least of their sins that they would talk Greek.

So English oath and Greek oath beat the air fruitlessly;

for the Greek could not understand the Epithet 'squint eyed monkey' nor could we interpret the vigour of his language; Greek we reflected is devoid of meaning. Action won the day: we turned our donkeys up the hill, & the Greeks gave in with more of laughter than anger. The Greek boys, in spite of the heat, ran & rolled, & chanted the odd wavering songs of the nation. Meanwhile we climbed, & touched the hill top after 5 hours or so. The view was worth much: directly beneath was Marathon, & Euboea; we could see Salamis, & the outlines of many promontories. The sea flowed everywhere. It was too late to stay, so we stumbled down again, by a path this time, leading through a valley sprinkled with black goats. The goatherd sat in his cloak by the wayside – demanded matches. The valley was sweet with thyme.

Marathon is as flat as a table, brown, with a perfect curve cut out of it by the bay. Small islands white as sand floated in the sea. Euboea is long & prominent, with bays scooped in the side. But there was little space for reflection!

From the quarry-stones of Pentelicus many of the greatest Greek buildings were made, and the mountain is scarred with workings. It is now also invested on all sides by the spread of Athenian suburbs – the monastery at its foot is surrounded by developments – and crowned by the installations of a radar station which keep the public from its summit, but look rather splendid, like the eyes of gods. The cave was probably the stalactite grotto at Spilia quarry, and its claim to fame was perhaps its early Christian associations. Virginia later wrote a laborious piece of fiction, A Dialogue upon Mount Pentelicus, *about their expedition up the mountain.*

At about 5 o'clock we had our last view of Athens, & its plain, & the famous hills. I have had reason to think of Athens only as a modern town, speaking a barbarous language, peopled by liars & cheats; as though to cancel that impression – to win back a faltering lover, albeit an insignificant one – the place seemed to glow once more in its beautiful old guise; the lights came trembling across the hills, & only the Acropolis was visible, standing high beyond the town. Stalwart & red & significant – alone & apart from all the modern world. To that then & the delicate impetuous hills, I could say farewell; for they are Greece, & so I have known them, & shall always know them.

On the Grand Tour II, *1932*

Twenty-six years later Virginia Woolf went back to Greece, this time with her husband Leonard and their friends Roger and Margery Fry, and sometimes, in visiting the same places as before, felt that she was meeting her own ghost, 'with all her life to come'. They travelled for the most part in a rented Hupmobile convertible, with chauffeur.

Greece then, so to return to Greece, is a land so ancient that it is like wandering in the fields of the moon. Life is receding . . . The living, these worn down, for ever travelling the roads Greeks, cannot master Greece any longer. It is too bare too stony, precipitous for them. We met them always on the high mountain passes padding along beside their donkeys, so small, existing so painfully, always marching in search of some herb, some root, mastered by the vast distances, unable to do more than dig their heels in the rock. Such solitude as they must know, under the sun, under the snow, such dependence on themselves to clothe & feed themselves through the splendid summer days is unthinkable in England. The centuries have left no trace. There is no 18th, 16th, 15th century all in layers as in England – nothing between them & 300 BC . . . If one finds a bay it is deserted; so too with the hills & valleys; not a villa, not a tea shop not a kennel anywhere; no wires, no churches, almost no graveyards.

Diary, 2 May

The roads are incredible – mere tracks between pits. We motor from dawn to dusk. Now we are at Delphi, with a torrent rushing down the street, 6 vultures, or golden eagles soaring above us, and whole sheep roasting over woodfires on poles because it is for some reason Easter Sunday. All the Greeks are therefore singing wild incantations and marching about with candles and corpses on biers. We have put Greek art in its place – rather lower than it was: on the other hand, their architecture is better than it was reputed. But the Byzantines are the real swells. (This is a quotation from Roger). Roger is a fair shower bath of erudition – Not a flower escapes him. And if it did, Margery would catch it. Between them every bird beast and stone is accounted for. We talk almost incessantly, and yesterday had the great joy of smelling a dead horse in a field. No sooner smelt than 12 – no – 15 vultures descended from the azure and proceeded to pick it. They have long blue bald necks like snakes. Sometimes a tortoise crosses the road – sometimes a lizard.

Roger is now hopelessly beaten. The Greeks are playing bagpipes and serenading the bleeding body of Christ in a very sensual minor key.

Letter to Quentin Bell, 1 May

Last night on the hill above Delphi in the evening light with Itea beginning to flash & sparkle by the sea, one ship in the bay & the snow mountains standing out in the background, & the foreground still running rich green & red brown, where the goats & sheep were grazing, & the cars passing slowly on the winding road beneath, last night as we sat there, the goat girl came bounding up as if to rick her sheep, but it was only to talk to us. No slinking past, no tittering, no shyness. She stopped before us, as a matter of course ... She shouted with laughter. She was small brown, will make a shrewd broad old woman; unconstrained, friendly ...

... They danced after dinner in the public house,

young men, punctiliously, bowing & twisting & keeping their feet on the right spot, dressed in trousers & shirts.

Diary, 2 May

Sometimes at weekends the shepherds, coming down from the mountains for refreshment, still dance in the evening at Delphi.

Roger had heard of a monastery [Hosios Loukas] with mosaics near Delphi – the driver pointed out that it would add 3 hours to our 10 hour journey, also climbing a mountain at midday on mules. Roger found a shorter way. But, the man said the road is impassable. Not a bit of it said Roger. So it was planned; and we got up at 5 ready to start. At the last moment news came that a car had rolled over the precipice owing to the bad road, and the driver abso-lutely refused to go. So we compromised and went the long way and rode up the hill in the heat of midday and the mosaics were very inferior and the Monks were very annoying, and we didn't get back to Athens till 8.30 at night, having broken a spring, punctured a tire, and run over a serpent. But we saw an eagle. And Roger said it was only by these experiments that one could get real insight into the people.

Letter to Vanessa Bell, 2 May

An excellent fast road now leads from Delphi to Hosios Loukas, which has lately been restored: its mosaics are more generally supposed to be very fine, its Monks are not at all annoying, its warnings about ladies wearing trousers are flexibly enforced and one can buy a cappuccino at a café in its courtyard.

Its Sunday at Athens; we've been lunching, not too well, and looking for 2 hours at Byzantine relics – because its a sultry wet day; and now we're off to Hymettus, and yester-day we went on a ship to Aegina, and saw the loveliest temple, and an island all carved in terraces with olives and wild flowers, and the sea running into the bays (it was pouring wet, I must admit, and we were herded with 50 American archaeologists) Still it is a beautiful island, and I padded to the hill top, picking wild irises and unknown yellow stars, and little purple, violet, blue, white, pearl flowers, all about as big as the stone on your ring no bigger. And we went to Daphnis, and wandered in olive woods, and to Sunium, the Temple on a cliff, which cliff is soft with flowers, all again no bigger than pearls or topazes. Margery Fry is a maniacal botanist, and squats – she's the size of a Russian bear – on the rocks digging with a penknife. And we saw the Greek shepherds huts in a wood near Marathon, and a lovely dark olive, red lipped, pink shawled girl wandering and spinning thread from a lump of wool from her own flock of sheep.

Letter to Vita Sackville-West, 24 April

Why did you never tell me that Greece was beautiful? Why did you never mention the sea and the hills and the valleys and the flowers? Am I the only person who has eyes in my head? I solemnly inform you, Ethel, that Greece is the most beautiful country in the whole world; May is the most beautiful season in the whole year; Greece and May to-gether —! There were the nightingales for example singing in the cypresses where we sat beside the stream: and I filled my lap with scarlet anemones; Yes, but you want facts; Baedeker. Well then, we went from Athens to Corinth; town being rebuilt after earthquake; gulf [canal] stopped owing to heavy fall of rock; six donkeys engaged in carting fall away; will take 6 months or year: all traffic meanwhile held up: Delphi cut off; oranges unobtainable in hotel: from Corinth (all this in a great open car of Giolmann's perfectly driven over roads like coagulated craters by en-chanting driver) to Mycenae: my word. magnificent. Bees booming in the Tomb of Agamemnon. (What is the line about 'his helmet made a hive for bees') tea at Belle Helene; among the plains, with frogs barking: so to Nauplia in the evenings; oh and then next day up the most nerve racking pass, shooting like an arrow along a razor with caverns of rock in abysses a million feet deep under one's left eye, and donkeys emerging round the corners to Mitrovitza; so to Mistra; Byzantine church magnificent; peasants delightful; coffee in a peasants room; so to Athens again; all the time the heat increasing and the wind, and the flowering trees visibly opening and making tassels of violet and white and crimson (dont ask me to document these facts) against a sky of flawless blue . . .

Letter to Ethel Smyth, 4 May

At La Belle Hélène Hotel, in Mycenae village (Schliemann's house during his epochal excavations in the 1870s) a reproduction of Virginia Woolf's signature in the register hangs on a wall, along with other famous names.

Greek Thoughts

🐾 I cant think why we dont live in Greece. Its very cheap. The exchange is now in our favour. There has been a financial crisis and we get I dont know how many shillings for our pound. The people are far the most sympathetic I've ever seen. Nobody jeers, or sneers. Everybody smiles. There are no beggars, practically. The peasants all come up across the fields and talk. We can't understand a word and the conflict between Roger's book and Leonards often makes it impossible for us to get a drop to drink, because they cant agree what is the word for wine.

Letter to Vanessa Bell, 2 May 1932

🐾 . . . The Ancient Greek had the best of it: we were very belated wayfarers: the shrines are fallen, & the oracles are dumb. You have the feeling very often in Greece – that the pageant has passed long ago, & you are come too late, & it matters very little what you think you feel. The modern Greece is so flimsy & fragile, that it goes to pieces entirely when it is confronted with the roughest fragments of the old.

Journal, September 1906

🖎 I can assure you Greece is more beautiful than 20 dozen Cambridges all in May week. It blazes with heat too, and there are no bugs, no inconveniences – the peasants are far nicer than the company we keep in London – its true we can't understand a word they say. In short I'm setting on foot a plan to remove the Hogarth Press to Crete.

Letter to John Lehmann, 8 May 1932

🖎 I bathed my feet in the Castalian spring [Delphi]; and all the rocks were covered with pale purple campanula – but whats the use of talking of flowers to an Englishwoman? You buy them in bunches: here they toss them at our heads. I've never seen so many – at Aegina yesterday the whole hill was red with rock roses, and yellow sea poppies, one of which I picked for you – here are its decaying petals. The sea gets in everywhere – you come to the top of a hill and there's the sea beneath. And snow mountains beyond, and bays as they were when Eve – no it should be Persephone – bathed there. Not a bungalow, not a kennel, not a tea shop. Pure sea water on pure sand is almost the loveliest thing in the world – you know how many times I've said so, and brought in old women with baskets. So yesterday we plunged into the sea and swam about in the Aegean, with sea urchins and anemones, all transmuted, waving red and yellow beneath our feet.

Letter to Vita Sackville-West, 8 May 1932

In 1992 the Castalian spring was closed to the public for rock stabilisation work (financed by the European Community), but its water is channelled through a nearby concrete conduit, and for Virginia's sake I washed my own feet in that.

🖎 . . . I looked up & saw mountains across the bay, knife shaped, coloured, & the sea, brimming smooth; & felt as if a knife had scraped some incrusted organ in me, for I could not find anything lacking in that agile, athletic beauty, steeped in colour, so that it was not cold, perfectly free from vulgarity, yet old in human life ... Now there are sympathies between people & places, as between human beings. And I could love Greece, as an old woman, so I think, as I once loved Cornwall, as a child.

Diary, 8 May 1932

Turkey

Virginia Woolf twice went to Turkey, and both visits were made unhappy by the illness en voyage of her sister Vanessa. In 1910 she made an emergency journey to Bursa, where Vanessa had suffered a miscarriage, in order to help her sister safely home to England; it was her only foray into Asia, but she wrote nothing about it. In 1906, when she had gone from Greece to Istanbul (then called Constantinople) with Vanessa, her brother Adrian and their friend Violet Dickinson, the visit was cut short by Vanessa's sickness, but this did not prevent Virginia, aged twenty-four, from keeping one of her wordier journals.

A Visit to Constantinople
Journal, October 1906

All day we have been steaming along the coast of Asia Minor, with an island springing now & then on our left. In the evening we stopped, in a neck of sea, commanded by great guns, where lies the famous town of the Dardanelles. A little further & we came to Abydos in Sestos, with the mound where Xerxes sat; his ghost might watch many strange passengers crossing from shore to shore. Shall we say that the coast of Asia Minor is like many another coast –

a faint dark streak, that swells & sinks, & is sprinkled here & there with white houses in clusters? And then you must add, to propitiate somebody or other, that we also passed the plain of Troy. But all that is too finely embedded in my mind to be extracted tonight. The good trustworthy ship plods on her way down the sea of Marmara & lets me write a neat hand, as though I bestrode a soft pacing nag.

When we wake at 5.30 we shall be exposed instantly to all the splendour of Constantinople.

And so we were, exposed, almost before our eyes were open. For waking at half past five I saw the land streaming past us, sharp black, with the pale lights of dawn upon the sea. At six I was on deck, & suddenly we found ourselves confronted with the whole of Constantinople; there was St Sophia, like a treble globe of bubbles frozen solid, floating out to meet us. For it is fashioned in the shape of some fine substance, thin as glass, blown in plump curves; save that it is also as substantial as a pyramid. Perhaps that may be its beauty. But then beautiful & evanescent & enduring, to pluck adjectives like black berries – as it is, it is but the fruit of a great garden of flowers. The sun was rising swiftly, opposite the town, & the whole sweep of grey houses piled high & curved freely was picked out lavishly & fantastically with golden windows. And so the colour was of gray houses, & pale golden panels, & dark tufts of green, for all the buildings were spaced with a soft fringe of trees. We passed rapidly before this wonderful sight, which seemed to renew itself afresh before our eyes, each instant, & so came to the crowded pool of the river, where the Golden Horn branches off from the Bosphorus. But here my point of view was certainly eclipsed; nor do I remember any more, as novelists say, & they have all the best devices – until – well, it would be convenient to say until about 6 o'clock in the evening, when I sat before an open window, & saw the sun set behind the town which had reflected its uprise.

From this position you see over the town, or as much

of it as a square window will compass, & that is enough to give you some idea that Constantinople is to begin with a very large town. Remembering Athens, you felt yourself in a metropolis; a place where life was being lived successfully. And that did seem strange, & – if I have time to say so – a little uncomfortable. For you also realised that life was not lived after the European pattern, that it was not even a debased copy of Paris or Berlin or London, & that, you thought was the ambition of towns which could not actually be Paris or any of those inner capitals. As the lights came out in clusters all over the land, & the water was busy with lamps, you knew yourself to be the spectator of a vigorous drama, acting itself out with no thought or need of certain great countries yonder to the west. And in all this opulence there was something ominous, & something ignominious – for an English lady at her bedroom window. At any rate, it was a stirring sight to look upon; & if I may use the shorthand of a hack writer, a most beautiful one into the bargain.

The Golden Horn drives a broad blue wedge between two high banks of houses; so that, as some one says, a battle ship rides at anchor in the street before your door. Then the sunset in long bars of flame & scarlet with a border of chimneys & mosques drawn black upon their lowest margin; the blue waters were lit up & golden lights were sprinkled upon them. Up in the air, & deep down in the earth the lamps burnt; & then the moon, a crescent, swung slowly up in the sky, & a pure drop of light, the evening star, turned the innumerable lamps to gold.

It was Alexander Kinglake, in his book Eōthen, *who made the remark about the battleship in the street.*

There are few experiences more exhilarating than the first dive into a new town – Even when your plunge is impeded – as ours was this morning – by a sleek Turkish dragoman. Still, when the driver cracked his whip, & the horses started down the hill, all our obstacles were forgotten. Innumerable pages have been turned in the history of Constantinople, but this, the last, was turned fresh for us. And yet, apart from the chafing of strange sights upon our senses, there was really nothing very memorable in our descent upon Stamboul. A view does not by any means promise beauty of detail; & the streets were insignificant, & the national dress – a fez & a frock coat – is a disappointing compromise. We reached a battered doorway, upon which there was some florid heraldry. 'The Sublime Porte' commented our guide, staying the carriage that we might do our homage. Beyond the gates the grass grew in the cobbles & a soldier lounged in a sentry box; imagination had done the work better already. Then at length we reached S. Sophia, by a narrow passage of paving stones, as though we approached by the back door. That little ceremony on the doorstep, when we cased our heretic leather in slippers, had a certain childlike pride in it. Travellers have made so much of the virtues of the change, considered aesthetically, that there is no longer any genuine interest in it. Perhaps it is a little game, kept alive for the amusement of the stranger & the profit of the native. At any rate we paid our tribute to the oriental superstition graciously, & shuffled in through the doors with lively satisfaction in our toes; But then I left half my tribute at an early stage, & defiled the carpet with stout English boots.

Perhaps this digression is artfully intended to reproduce here something of the hesitation which made my mind also waver from the business in hand at this point. Here was St. Sophia; & here was I, with one brain 2 eyes, legs & arms in proportion, set down to appreciate it. Now what ever impression it made was certainly fragmentary & inconsequent; as thus – strange rays of light, octagonal & colourless; windows without stained glass; no screen across the church; & was it a church? No; it was a great hall of business, or learning or law; for it was empty & circular, & the flagged pavement was covered with carpets. There were men in turbans squatting together at one end; they

rose & went away, talking loudly, when their conclave was
finished. There were many single figures wandering up &
down the great open space, reflectively; there were one or
two who, seated at the side, rocked their bodies rhyth-
mically to the tune of the Koran spread open upon their
knees. Here was a group with white turbans from Bokhara;
the guide did not scruple to elbow his way through their
devotions, nor did they mind the interruption. Such were
the worshippers in the mosque of S. Sophia; nor did their
worship seem inappropriate to the place. It is so large, & so
secular, so little the precinct of an awful religion that this
miscellaneous worship did not offend it. Nor did the great
place strike one as 'beautiful'; for though there are patches
of mosaic left upon the arches, the zeal of the Turks has
stripped the temple bare of ornament. A Turk may not see
the sign of the Cross at his prayer or that prayer fades into
mist said our guide, with a wave of his hand; & rather than
nullify his devotions the decoration of the whole building
had been corrected & erased altogether till it has no virtue
or vice left in it. Crosses have become safe patterns without
meaning; sacred heads have been obliterated from the wall,
& shields of wood proclaim the true faith where Christian
angels used to spread their wings. There is a niggardly
temper in all this that makes the great mosque not very
sympathetic to the stranger; although to qualify my blame,
there is much that cannot avoid being uttered in honest
admiration.

If it is not a temple of religion as we understand the
word it is surely a temple of something; so much you may
read in the fanatic nodding of so many turbans, & the
earnest drone of so many voices.

The last thing, as it is generally the first, that such super-
ficial travellers as I am should enter in their note books is
the state of a people's religion. Indeed the only remark I
can make with any confidence is that no Christian, or even
European, can hope to understand the Turkish point of

view; you are born Christians or Mahommedans as surely as you are born black or white. The difference is in the blood that beats in the pulse. And that difference was stated explicitly when we took our seats this evening in the gallery of S. Sophia. We gazed as we might have gazed at creatures behind a cage; only the truth was that these creatures were neither our captives nor our inferiors; they suffered us to watch them, but they would not suffer us to pray with them.

We climbed the long slant that leads to the top of the church, & half way up we heard shrill cries echoing in a great space, like the cries of many children, let out of school. And when we looked down into the church there were troops of children, who played hide & seek among the august pillars, & chattered like monkeys as they ran.

Their voices sounded thin & even plaintive as they floated up through vast depths of yellow air. But no cry could disturb the serenity of that great hall. Rings of hanging light made little islands in the immense gloom; & gradually, as the lamps were lit all round the arches, a soft golden glow shone forth from ceiling & column, till the air seemed warmed to the core. The hall began to fill with dark figures, & the children were hushed, though they flitted in & out like soft bats. And all the while the light grew slowly brighter, till the line of all the stately arches filled in the picture. Meanwhile the people took their places in rows along the mats, & you heard a voice rising & falling, with sacred words. The air was crowded, & yet you could hardly distinguish separate figures; only you had the feeling that at the bottom of this vague amber coloured air multitudes were gathered together, slumped like shadows.

The voice seemed but a thin thread to unite so many bodies; but at certain moments all the long lines rose & fell simultaneously, kissed the floor, & stood upright again, the puppets of an unseen power.

The circles of light were dim, & the whole of this punctual action was carried on in the twilight, silently with only one voice sounding plaintively alone. But simple & melan-

choly as the ceremony seemed to us, it was also wonderfully beautiful. The subtle lights, which were all woven of
burnished golds & soft blacks, poured over all & revealed
nothing thin or harsh; they revealed nothing but suggested
more than can be drawn forth. So we watched, a scene
which we shall never understand; & heard the true gospels
expounded in an unknown tongue.

The mystery of the sight, & the strangeness of the
voice, made you feel yourself like one wrapped in a soft
curtain; & the worshippers within are quite determined
that you shall remain outside.

On the third or the fourth day it is well to leave all duties
undone, in order that you may lose your way in the unrecorded slums. Here even a stranger & a tourist may
stumble upon something that is quite without self con-
sciousness; & then the town for the first time will become a
real town of flesh & blood.

That part of the prescription which consists of losing
yourself we followed very carefully; & we had the delight
of walking streets that led nowhere just because we
chanced to find ourselves in their path. Now in the purlieus
of Constantinople a great deal of the Gorgeous East still
runs warm; a vine was laced across the road, & a various
torrent of red fezes, turbans, yashmaks, & European respectability came pouring down it, like a turbulent
Highland water. But no one stopped to look at us, & the
eccentricities of all our dresses seemed but part of the
ordinary composition.

We had to find a Bazaar, the Grand Bazaar indeed, & in
time, after mingling with all this busy & happy life, we took
refuge in a great honeycomb of little shops, built beneath a
single roof & divided into streets & alleys like the ways of a
city of dwelling houses. To buy, it is necessary to be pos-
sessed of infinite time, & infinite duplicity. The silks were
ruinous, they were hideous; in England you might buy
them for half the price; still the fact remained explain it

how you would that we wished to buy, & were extrava-
gantly prepared to pay the sum of 4 piastres a pique – the
English are a great and generous race.

Did he hear aright? Could anyone make such an offer
seriously? No, it was an insult to our intelligence to suppose
that we could so misjudge the excellence of Broussa silk –
An American might be thus ignorant – but in England taste
& knowledge surely forbids. And did Monsieur on his part,
so grievously misunderstand his own interests as to charge
the English more than it was right to pay? There were
ladies willing to buy in the hotel; but such a price would
amaze them. Something of this kind did get itself translated
into French, & interpreted into Turkish, & at intervals of 15
minutes a piastre was dropped from the price; till the pro-
cess of squeezing could be carried no further without
encroaching on that halfpenny worth of profit which alone
remained, & without making us still more late for our tea.
But I have little doubt that the shop keeper had a right to
smile over his plump cigarette.

*The Grand Bazaar (Kapali Carsi) contained at that time some
7,000 shops, stalls and ateliers, and probably has about the same
number today. In them, so Virginia's accounts show, she bought
for herself cloaks (£1 5s.), silk (4s. 2d.) and Turkish delight
(1s. 4d.): her brother Adrian bought a pair of scissors.*

The Turks have undoubtedly one valuable gift, which is the
gift of names. 'The Golden Horn' has whispered sweetly in
ears that never left London; & to wake the imagination is
half the battle, where places are concerned. Certainly, the
actual waters are a little disappointing as the real thing
must always be, bends the figure of the thing, for it is
almost blasphemous to test any place as crudely as we
tested the Golden Horn today. We paid our fare & took a
penny steamboat upon its very waters. It is not much different in beauty from other rivers that pass through other
towns; certainly the houses on the bank are less regular, &

the traffic on the stream is more various & vivacious. Also you have shaven green down for background, which comes running to the waters edge here & there, & the prospect – half closing ones eyes – is perhaps as gay & happy as such sights can be. But on the whole the most splendid thing in Constantinople – this is the verdict of a three day old tourist – is the prospect of the roofs of the town, seen from the high ground of Pera. For in the morning a mist lies like a veil that muffles treasures across all the houses & all the mosques; then as the sun rises, you catch hints of the heaped mass within; then a pinnacle of gold pierces the soft mesh, & you see shapes of precious stuff lumped together. And slowly the mist withdraws, & all the wealth of gleaming houses & rounded mosques lies clear on the solid earth, & the broad waters run bright as daylight through their midst. It is such a sight as you can watch at all hours, for it is so large & simple that the eye has always much to speculate upon; & there is no need to compose it with careful forefinger.

Constantinople is a place of live nerves, & taut muscles; so we read directly we saw the town laid at our feet; but continuing the metaphor we also said that the eyes of this great giantess were veiled.

The streets & bridges are crowded with men & women, horses & carriages; here is an English diplomat & here a lean native, who proposes to start a pilgrimage in a fortnights time for Mecca. A sleek merchant hustles him on his way to his office; but nevertheless he understands; the two may meet on the same praying rug at sundown.

There is faith enough; & business enough; & life enough to keep both eddying swiftly along the stream. No one who has visited the Mosques & the bazaars can doubt the force of the current. But at the same time, no one knows exactly where it tends; a dozen stories of the place show that it can take a subterranean channel, & it was not ten years ago that the Turks & Armenians massacred each other in the streets. So perhaps if it were your lot to spend your life here you might think your station one of some risk – as a resting place beneath a volcano. Happily a traveller need not trouble himself with the intricate roots of all these strange separate flowers that we look at above ground. The strangeness is attractive; & then the town upon which the drama is played is fair enough for any tragedy.

But can we make this plain on a white sheet of paper? You must remember not only the morning veil of mist, & the stately domes that shine through, & all the gold & white & blue of the town at midday, but you must think also of the little streets crowded with live people, you must re- member the turbans & the veiled women, the arab horses & the yellow dogs . . .

As for those observations upon manners or politics with which all travellers should ballast their impressions, I con- fess I find myself somewhat out of pocket today. The truth is that travellers deal far too much in such commodities, & my efforts to rid myself of certain preconceptions have taken my attention from the actual facts. Were we not told for instance, that the female sex was held of such small account in Constantinople – or rather it was so strictly guarded – that a European lady walking unveiled might have her boldness rudely chastised? But the streets are full of single European ladies, who pass unmarked; & that veil which we heard so much of – because it was typical of a dif- ferent stage of civilisation & so on – is a very frail symbol. Many native women walk bare faced; & the veil when worn is worn casually, & cast aside if the wearer happens to be curious. But it does have so much virtue in it as to sug- gest that it hides something rare & spotless, so that you gaze all the more at a forbidden face. And then the passionate creature raises her shield for a moment – & you see – a benevolent old spinster, with gold rims to spectacles, trot- ting out to buy a fowl for dinner. What danger has she got to hide from? Whom would a sight of her face seduce?

The men save for their red caps & an occasional nose like a scimitar, might be citizens of London, save that the breezes of the Bosporus have tanned their skin & expanded their chests. But their faces are reserved; & that is the real mark of a civilised people. They have something to think about, & you can pass the time without the help of speech. And more over they are courteous to strangers, & will offer you fragments of many different languages in order that you may choose your own.

But when we come to consider the question of the West & the East – then indeed – we lay down the pen, & write no more.

Exotica

Culture Shocks

🐦 We've been in Holland, Germany and Italy, and seen ever so many different civilizations; in fact my brain is so crowded I want to subside into a coma, like a spinning top and cease spinning.

Letter to Victoria O'Campo, 28 May 1935, from Moulins, France

🐦 I am half dazed with travelling, so many cities I have seen, and smelt: now its the waves breaking, and the scent of stocks in the garden – and there is very likely a nightingale, and frogs ... We're so brown cheeked red nosed and altogether dusty shaggy shabby ...

Letter to Vita Sackville-West, 20 May 1933, from Spotorno, Italy

🐦 We have seen vultures, buzzard, eagles, bee eaters, blue thrushes, temples, ruins, statues, Athens, Sparta, Corinth – and are just off to a monastery. So goodbye.

Letter to Julian Bell, 5 May 1932, from Athens

🐦 Then Roger shouts, Oh come and look at this! My word thats swell – very swell – and we all gaze up ... at some annunciation or Crucifixion: and I steal away to the marble door and see the olives and the pines baring their heads and letting the sun and shade darken and illumine them and think how theyre like waves on the grey hill side.

Letter to Ethel Smyth, 4 May 1932, from Athens

Religion

I like the Roman Catholic religion. I say it is an attempt at art; Leonard is outraged – We burst into a service of little girls in white veils this morning which touched me greatly. It seems to me simply the desire to create gone slightly crooked, and no God in it at all. Then there are little boys brandishing palms tied in red ribbon and sugar lambs everywhere – surely rather sympathetic.

Letter to Vanessa Bell, 9 April 1927, from Palermo

At night, in the still heat, we stood on the balcony and saw the procession go by, singing in a minor key some, to me, impressive and solemn dirge round a bier; and the clergy with beards and long hair and still catafalque like robes sang, and I can assure you that all that is in me of stunted and deformed religion flowered under this hot sensuality, so thick, so yellow, so waxen ... Why, we almost wept, we pagans.

Letter to Ethel Smyth, 4 May 1932, from Athens

I'm sitting at a courtyard at an Inn table, with the Feast of St John going on – that is gypsies dancing, old men in black velvet suits with silver buttons, divine youths in mediaeval doublets, girls with lace caps like the Eiffel tower dancing ... They strew the streets with branches and flowers, and we saw an archbishop – a man clad all in white samite under a palanquin of gold and stars – blessing a fishing boat slung with roses today against a lead blue sea. Its certainly a great advantage to have a reason for dressing up.

Letter to Vanessa Bell, 18 June 1939, from Bayeux

Hotels

This hotel . . . to be brutal & candid, is not to be recommended, although it would be scarcely fair to abuse it.

It has a strange likeness to a shabby English public house, of the early days of the nineteenth century. Prince Albert & a fat deer might hang above the side board, & there is the mahogany table all ready for the keepsakes & the bibles. Mild respectable people who wish for a quiet dinner come here & breathe congenial air in the long dismal dining room. There is a great table, spread with cold silver baskets, & laid with accurate covers for the guests who never come. We dine in furtive corners, as though our needs were too modest to require a dinner table, & certainly all our cheer such as it is, is not sufficient to kindle the vaporous room.

Journal, Constantinople, 1906

Miss Cotton . . . finds she can live at Diano Marina for 8/- a day . . . It was Liberty Hall here . . . Meanwhile there came in the 2 guests [?] in evening dress, the deaf lady & the voluble; also the powdered white lady with the red scarf: & after dinner – they often give us asparagus, she said – & they had their own bottles of wine – the two parties settled in at their own tables . . . & played bridge. Now this half pay spinster will dwindle on, beside the sea under the mountain, chatting, till she dies.

Diary, 11 May 1933, at Rapallo

A secondrate inn in Draguinan – with plane trees outside, the usual single noted bird, the usual loudspeaker . . . The hotel keepers are gorged, & scarcely stop playing cards.

Diary, 21 May 1933

We are both burnt bright brick red; we are both slightly tipsy . . . Happily we have pitched on a purely Italian inn – rather humble; W.C.'s fair; no English spoken, and we sit drinking coffee with Italian sailors and officers after dinner.

Letter to Angus Davidson, 14 April 1927, from Syracuse, Sicily

There is a strange race that haunts Hotels – gnome like women, who are like creatures that come out in the dark. An hotel is a sort of black cave. This one is really very good of its kind.

Letter to Emma Vaughan, 25 April 1904, from the Palace Hotel, Florence

Here we are, safe, ever so cold, shivering and shaking with cold . . . The hotels at night are getting rather a trial. No central heating; or the machine failed. We sit under the one light, wrapped in a rug, as now: try to read; get into bed about 9; and then there's a movie next door – tonight a wedding. They've been dancing since 5 . . . Lord – but the noise they make!

Letter to Vita Sackville-West, 28 April 1931, from Dreux, France

In every hotel in Ireland sits a military man with poached egg eyes & sandy hair, a loud commanding voice, & sponge-bag coat & red slippers, after a day's fishing. There he sits & drinks; & all day he fishes . . . And thats what Ireland is kept for: in every place where there's a river is built a large Inn, with town cooking & hot water & ladies & gentlemen's lavatories, though there's nothing but bog & hill for miles around, & there in the lounge the majors sit, & pay for the fishing, while the natives talk & talk & talk – about the old Kings of Ireland, presumably.

Diary, 8 May 1934

The usual small French inn, with farmers lunching . . . We began with paté of duck, went on to trout, gnocchi, stuffed chicken and spinach made with cream and then sour cream and a delicious cake and then pears *ad lib* . . . the vastest and most delicious meal I have ever eaten.

Letter to Leonard Woolf, 27 September 1928, from Avallon, France

The fire burnt in the middle of the room, and the company of Spanish peasants sat round and drank and stared at us, and we expected to have knives in our throats every moment. Then we were given one room – the only sleeping room – with one bed – and a canvas door between us and the family who undressed outside, and we locked our door as best we could – and lay down delicately side by side in our clothes, and heard the old woman counting her money, and swearing and spitting, and by degrees we went to sleep, and at 9 they brought us goats milk, and told us to get up and be gone.

Letter to Violet Dickinson, 24 April 1905, about an inn in Andalusia

On the Road

This is the way to live, I can assure you. Driving all day; an hour or two for lunch: a few churches perhaps to be seen; one's inn at night: wine, dinner; bed; off again – gradually it gets Southern, and we take off our jerseys and I have had to buy a silk one. One drops in upon people playing dominoes in cafés: or one stops on a mountain, and I sit on a stone, and L. tries to discover why the umbrella leaks at the nose.

Letter to Vita Sackville-West, 21 March 1928, from Orange, France

I've always been here before in trains – you cant think what a difference it makes driving, or being driven. We stop or go on; and have our lunch under cypresses, with nightingales singing and frogs barking, and climb to the top of hills where no one has ever been before. They are charming people – the peasants, I mean: very melancholy, longing for conversation, offering one wine, or 6 dead fish – I've only 10 words of Italian, but I fire them all perpetually; and so we get led into all kinds of queer places.

Letter to Elizabeth Bowen, 16 May 1933, from Siena, Italy

On the Ferry

. . . We crossed over to Palermo by night and I shared a cabin with an unknown but by no means romantic Swedish lady who complained that there was no lock on the door, whereupon I poked my head out from the curtains and said in my best French 'Madame, we have neither of us any cause for fear' which happily she took in good part.

Letter to Vanessa Bell, 9 April 1927

Out of the Train Window

Looking out of the carriage window at Civita Vecchia, whom should we see, sitting side by side on a bench, but D. H. Lawrence and Norman Douglas – unmistakable: Lawrence pierced and penetrated; Douglas hog-like and brindled – They were swept off by train one way and we went on to Rome.

Letter to Vanessa Bell, 9 April 1927

On the Orient Express

Only the most hardened scribbler could attempt to write in the Orient Express ... Last night was bad. Very hot. Then interruptions. At Salonika (1.30) they came in to ask about money. We had been advised to hide all except 600 drachmas – where? In the electric light bell he said. An impossible idea – so we disposed them all over – in the pockets of Baedeker, in an envelope.

Diary, 10 May 1932

The Price of Travel

And so down to Parma; hot, stony, noisy; with shops that dont keep maps; & so along a racing road to Piacenza, at which we find ourselves now at 6 minutes to 9 P.M. This of course is the rub of travel – this is the price paid for the sweep & the freedom – the dusting of our shoes & careering off tomorrow – & eating our lunch on a green plot beside a

deep cold stream . . . Comfort and discomfort; & the zest &
rush that no engagements, hours, habits give.

Diary, 19 May 1933

A Halt in Belgrade

 We went out in the rain & walked up the broad stucco
streets . . . we saw nothing but very tall men in tight fitting
clothes: two women in looping breeches & Turkish handkerchiefs; & so back to the train again.

Diary, 11 May 1932

Sturm und Drang in Greece

A storm rushed up from the Aegean, black as arrows,
and the blue was as blue as hard china, and the storm and
the blue fell upon each other and 10 million German
tourists rushed across the temple precisely like suppliants in
their grey and purple mackintoshes.

Letter to Vita Sackville-West, 24 April 1932

Night in Turkey

Waking at night – & the dogs are good watchmen, you
hear a soft funereal sound, like that which mourns over the
graves of soldiers. It is the beat of a muffled drum, rhyth-
mical & regular, which neither sinks nor rises nor passes on
its way. Yet it is three o'clock in the morning. Soon a chant
rises in the lull between beats, a priest, you fancy, chanting
the dirge over the body that is thus lamented. Again some
metallic instrument chimes against the soft thud of the
drum.

Journal, October 1906

Italian Mountains

Of the Apennines I have nothing to say — save that up on the top theyre like the inside of a green umbrella: spine after spine: & clouds caught on the point of the stick.

Diary, 19 May 1933

The Mediterranean

Purple brown sea, not rolling in waves . . . but now and then giving a little shiver, like that which runs through a field of corn, or the back of a race horse . . . Hills like songs, like poems, thought of all in one flash and for ever.

Letter to Ethel Smyth, 18 May 1933, from Lerici

Foreign Ways

How much more enjoyable in some queer way France is than England! But how does one learn the language? I must and will. I want to know how the French think. After the English, they seem so natural, so much akin to all one likes.

Letter to Jacques Raverat, 30 March 1923

& all the men go into the urinal, one sees their legs; & the Morocco soldiers go in their great cloaks; & the children play ball, & people stand lounging, & everything becomes highly pictorial, composed, legs, in particular — the odd angles they make, & the people dining in the hotel; & the queer air it all has . . .

Diary, 23 May 1933, in Vienne, France

Foreign Looks

Yes, I thought: I will make a note of that face — the face of the woman stitching a very thin, lustrous green silk at a table in the restaurant where we lunched at Vienne. She was like fate – a consummate mistress of all the arts of self preservation: hair rolled & lustrous; eyes so nonchalant; nothing could startle her; there she sat stitching her green silk with people coming & going all the time; she not looking, yet knowing, fearing nothing, expecting nothing – a perfectly equipped middle class French woman.

Diary, 9 May 1933

I haven't seen one German woman who has a face; they are puddings of red dough, and they dress in high art colours, with symbolical embroideries, rather like old Irish jewels, in their backs.

Letter to Vanessa Bell, 12 August 1909

Foreign Advantages

I am amazed that we should live in England and order dinner every morning . . . and catch trains when we might roll in bliss every moment of the day and sit and drink coffee on a balcony overlooking lemon trees and orange trees with mountains behind and every sort of colour and shade perpetually changing . . . then a delicious lunch off rice and bacon and olive oil and onions and figs and sugar mixed, then off to a place where cypresses and palm trees grow together.

Letter to Roger Fry, 16 April 1923, from Murcia, Spain

Envoi

In the course of editing this book I have followed Virginia Woolf's trail wherever she went, and I have found her shade oddly equivocal. Sometimes she is vividly remembered, sometimes utterly forgotten, and sometimes she has become a kind of myth.

At Cassis in France my hotel receptionist knew exactly where Virginia had stayed, and in the New Forest a passer-by accurately directed me to the house at Lyndhurst, miles away, where she spent two fairly miserable Christmases. Every year hundreds of pilgrims visit Talland House at St Ives, lured there by the magic of *To the Lighthouse*. Scholars, students, film-makers and plain readers are constant callers at Fontecreuse, the cradle of *The Waves*.

Elsewhere, on the other hand, I found people surprised to learn that Virginia Woolf had ever been there at all – in Galway City, for instance, a very literary town too, and in Bayreuth. Hoteliers were often gratified to discover that she could be listed among their clientele: householders more delighted still, to know that she had once slept in their bedrooms.

Seldom in the course of my enquiries did I meet people who had never heard of Virginia Woolf: but sometimes I found her identity was blurred or legendary, somewhere between fact and fiction, and more than once my respondents, remembering only the film of Edward Albee's play *Who's Afraid of Virginia Woolf?*, replied simply to my enquiries: 'Wasn't that the one Elizabeth Taylor was in?'

I cannot pretend that when I undertook the work I was among Virginia Woolf's greatest admirers. Some of her novels I have never been able to enjoy (notably *The Waves*, generally supposed to be her greatest). More to the point, I despised what I heard of her snobbery, condescension and habits of social intimidation. I did not much like the sound of the Bloomsbury set that surrounded her, and I had been antagonised by the feminist gush and academic pedantry that attended her memory.

In the course of the task, however, I found my attitude reversed, for in reading all Virginia Woolf's diaries and letters I unearthed, beneath the public image, a personality I grew truly fond of. As I journeyed around Europe with her, this other Virginia constantly made me laugh, captivated me with the pithiness of her judgements, disarmed me by her taste for fun, moved me by her affinity with pathos and her way with animals and children. One could hardly ask for a better travelling companion. It seems to me that the more private she was – the less shy, in fact – the more enchanting she became: the more intimate and natural her relationships, the less daunting.

If she is forgotten in so many of the places she visited, she was always vividly present to me. Fortunately I was accompanying her only in the happier moments of her life – her periodic lapses into madness did not happen during her travels. Nevertheless I felt her beside me most powerfully of all at the place where, on 28 March 1941, home from her travels at Rodmell in Sussex, she ended her own life.

Monk's House at Rodmell is now a property of the National Trust, and there the whole world visits Virginia in her writing-hut at the end of the garden. Below the house a rough track runs through water-meadows to the River Ouse, and one afternoon I followed it with Virginia Woolf on her last journey. It is a curiously unkempt piece of country – gypsy country, with ponies about, and a shed with chickens, and scattered flood-protection works. It is further than one thinks from the house to the river, and all the way down I felt beside me that slender agitated figure, in one of the long skirts she preferred, wearing a hat I imagined, with a walking-stick in her hand, her mind full of words and racing thoughts – speaking them aloud perhaps, as she ran and stumbled down the track.

The place where she died is not a very lovely spot, for the river there has been artificially embanked, and there are warning notices of one kind and another, and a hut or two. I said goodbye to her there, though, with no sense of sadness. I felt she was being liberated at last permanently into that world of light, merriment and sympathy which was the half-hidden landscape of her genius, and through which I had travelled with her so delightfully.

Acknowledgements

Acknowledgements are due to the editors of the following works which have proved invaluable:

A Passionate Apprentice: The Early Journals of Virginia Woolf, edited by Mitchell A. Leaska, The Hogarth Press, 1990.

The Diary of Virginia Woolf, 5 volumes, edited by Anne Olivier Bell assisted by Andrew McNeillie, The Hogarth Press, 1977-84.

A Moment's Liberty: The Shorter Diary of Virginia Woolf, edited and abridged by Anne Olivier Bell, The Hogarth Press, 1990.

The Letters of Virginia Woolf, 6 volumes, edited by Nigel Nicolson assisted by Joanne Trautmann Banks, The Hogarth Press, 1975-1980.

Congenial Spirits: The Selected Letters of Virginia Woolf, edited by Joanne Trautmann Banks, The Hogarth Press, 1989.

The Essays of Virginia Woolf, volumes 1-3, edited by Andrew McNeillie, The Hogarth Press, 1986-1988.

Virginia Woolf: A Biography, Quentin Bell, The Hogarth Press, published in 2 volumes, 1972; in 1 volume, 1982, 1990.

Index

The Virginia Woolf Collection

HARDBACK FICTION

ISBN	TITLE	PRICE
0701209046	Hogarth Collected Edition	£125.91
0701208805	Between the Acts	£13.99
0701208791	Jacob's Room	£13.99
0701208821	Mrs Dalloway	£13.99
0701208775	Night and Day	£13.99
0701208740	Orlando	£13.99
0701208783	To the Lighthouse	£13.99
0701208813	The Voyage Out	£13.99
0701208767	The Waves	£13.99
0701208759	The Years	£13.99
070120852X	The Complete Shorter Fiction	£20.00

PAPERBACK FICTION

ISBN	TITLE	PRICE
0701209917	Between the Acts	£6.99
0701209925	Jacob's Room	£6.99
0701209933	Mrs Dalloway	£6.99
0701209941	Night and Day	£6.99
0701209968	To the Lighthouse	£6.99
0701209976	The Voyage Out	£6.99
0701209984	The Waves	£6.99
0701200230	The Years	£6.99
070120995X	Orlando	£6.99

NON-FICTION

ISBN	TITLE	PRICE
0701209461	Flush	£5.99pbk
0701209488	Roger Fry	£7.99pbk
070120947X	A Room of One's Own	£5.99pbk
0701209496	Three Guineas	£5.99pbk

LETTERS

ISBN	TITLE	PRICE
0701204486	Vol.IV A Reflection of the Other Person	£20.00
0701204699	Vol.V The Sickle Side of the Moon	£20.00
0701208651	Congenial Spirits: Selected Letters	£20.00

LETTERS (contd.)

0701209828	Congenial Spirits: Selected Letters	£10.99pbk
070120950X	Vol.I The Flight of the Mind	£12.99pbk
0701210303	Vol.II The Question of Things Happening	£12.99pbk
0701210311	Vol.III A Change of Perspective	£12.99pbk
070121032X	Vol.IV A Reflection of the Other Person	£12.99pbk
0701210338	Vol.V The Sickle Side of the Moon	£12.99pbk
0701210346	Vol.VI Leave the Letters Till We're Dead	£12.99pbk

DIARIES

0701204249	Vol. I	£20.00
0701204478	Vol. II	£20.00
0701204664	Vol. III	£20.00
0701208449	A Moment's Liberty: Shorter Diary	£20.00
0701209836	A Passionate Apprentice: Early Journals	£12.99pbk

ESSAYS

0701206667	Vol. I	£25.00
0701206675	Vol. II	£25.00
0701206683	Vol. III	£25.00
0701206691	Vol. IV (due 1994)	£25.00

All prices are subject to alteration
without prior notice.